A SINGER'S
EPIPHANY

FAITH, MUSIC, AND MORTALITY

A SINGER'S EPIPHANY

FAITH, MUSIC, AND MORTALITY

Lynn Eustis

FOREWORD BY
LOIS SVARD

GIA Publications, Inc.
Chicago, IL

A Singer's Epiphany:
Faith, Music, and Mortality
Lynn Eustis

G-10288

ISBN 978-1-62277-489-0

GIA Publications, Inc.
7404 S. Mason Ave.
Chicago, IL 60638
www.giamusic.com

Edited by Kirin Nielsen.
Cover and layout design by Martha Chlipala.
Printed in the United States of America.

The Things That Count

Now, dear, it isn't the bold things,
Great deeds of valour and might,
That count the most in the summing up of life at the end of the day.
But it is the doing of old things,
Small acts that are just and right;
And doing them over and over again, no matter what others say;
In smiling at fate, when you want to cry, and in keeping at work
    when you want to play—
Dear, those are the things that count.

And, dear, it isn't the new ways
Where the wonder-seekers crowd
That lead us into the land of content, or help us to find our own.
But it is keeping to true ways,
Though the music is not so loud,
And there may be many a shadowed spot where we journey along
    alone;
In flinging a prayer at the face of fear, and in changing into a song a
    groan—
Dear, these are the things that count.

My dear, it isn't the loud part
Of creeds that are pleasing to God,

Not the chant of a prayer, or the hum of a hymn, or a jubilant shout
 or song.
But it is the beautiful proud part
Of walking with feet faith-shod;
And in loving, loving, loving through all, no matter how things go
 wrong;
In trusting ever, though dark the day, and in keeping your hope
 when the way seems long—
Dear, these are the things that count.

Ella Wheeler Wilcox

Contents

Foreword
by Lois Svard

For musicians, music is not simply a job, a profession, or what we do. Music is who we are. Most of us have been singing or playing an instrument from an early age and practicing for several hours a day nearly every day of our lives. We bring the totality of our life experiences, our learning, our attitudes, our fears into every performance we give and every lesson we teach. Or as Nadia Boulanger—the great French composer, conductor, and teacher—once said, "Music can never be more or less than who you are as a human being."

But who are we when our brain, the organ that controls everything we do as a musician and everything about who we are as a person, goes rogue? In this moving and insightful memoir, Lynn Eustis explores what it means to be a professional musician and teacher at the height of her career who is suddenly faced with a brain tumor, a tumor that not only threatens her life, but upends her concept of who she is.

Near the end of this book, Eustis writes, "It is easy to let our concept of time be overtaken by a large, stressful event, and to forget all of the many smaller gifts that make up the daily movie of our lives." The reader is introduced to the stressful event, the abnormality in Eustis's brain, in the first sentence in Chapter 1 of *A Singer's*

Epiphany. Based on the journal writings she kept throughout this experience, Eustis shares her journey in this book as she reacquaints herself and the reader with the many smaller things that make a life worth living.

I met Lynn when she was a second-year college student and I was a first-year university professor. She was a voice performance major, and I taught piano which she also studied. We bonded during her lessons as we talked about what matters most in music, communicating the emotional content of the music, and also over discussions of what it means to be an independent woman in the professional music world. What I remember most about Lynn from that time was her fierce determination to rise to any musical challenge; her kindness to, and empathy for fellow students who may be going through a difficult time; and her dry and sometimes unexpected sense of humor.

Those qualities are here in abundance in her memoir. She invites the reader into her relationships with her doctors, her students, her family, her friends, and her faith, as she navigates the diagnosis of the tumor, the surgery, and treatment, and finding a way to move forward in this new, unexpected, and uncharted life. We see her rising to yet one more challenge, although of a markedly different dimension than any faced previously. And as with previous challenges, she faces the diagnosis and treatment with steely determination, returning to the concert stage within weeks after brain surgery. Her humor remains intact as she tries to elicit a smile from an unsmiling doctor. And she remains committed to, and concerned about, her students and how her illness may impact them.

Musicians are great at pumping ourselves up for the next performance or event: "The show must go on," "No pain, no gain," "Break a leg," "Sing your heart out." We are accustomed to forging through, no matter what. But the music profession is slowly coming to realize something the sports world has recognized for decades.

Musicians have unique health issues related to the lives they lead, the hours of practicing, and the stress of performance. Today, nearly every professional music organization devotes time to addressing the impact on musicians of hearing health, vocal health, mental health, and anatomical health. A growing body of journal articles, books, and webinars speaks to various aspects of a musician's health and well-being in a field that is known for physical and mental stress.

But to my knowledge, no one has addressed what it means to be a musician diagnosed with a brain tumor, or, for that matter, cancer in general. Many people turn to music to help them heal when faced with a traumatic event. But what happens when it is the person making the music who is dealt the devasting medical diagnosis? Since musicians tend to equate our personal and our musical selves, what does it mean when this organ that controls both our mind and body, and therefore our music making, goes its own way and develops a tumor? How does it affect one's performance and one's teaching? And who are we if we aren't making music?

Lynn's poignant memoir is important for anyone who values making music who has faced a life-threating or brain-threatening event in their lives. Her account of how to find the way forward in one's performance, teaching, and life is told with uncompromising honesty, vulnerability, and humor. Her steely determination allows her to not let cancer define her, but to lead her to a more authentic way of defining her own relationship with performance, her students, and herself, and to finding "the many smaller gifts that make up the daily movie of our lives."

—Lois Svard, DMA
author of the blog *The Musician's Brain*

Introduction

In the Japanese art of *kintsugi*, the cracks in damaged pottery are filled with gold-dusted lacquer in order to transform the imperfections into a newly beautiful work of art. *Kintsugi* is considered a perfect example of *wabi-sabi*, the traditional Japanese aesthetic defined as an acceptance of transience and imperfection. It is an embrace of beauty that is imperfect, impermanent, and incomplete. According to *wabi-sabi*, we should focus on the blessings hiding in our daily lives and celebrate the way things are rather than worry about the way we think things should be.

Sometimes in life we are shown how much more beautiful our lives are after the major cracks appear. Terrible things happen to people every day in this world, and sometimes the cracks are never filled. I believe that most people, faced with personal breakage, are given ways to bind themselves together and to find joy in an exquisite new life.

I was diagnosed in January 2014 with a brain tumor, an unexpected and unwelcome imperfection. I endured brain surgery and months of treatment, all of which led me to a crisis of identity. Would I recover? How long did I have? Would I be the same person on the other side, assuming I made it out of this at least for a while?

The answer to the last question is a resounding "no." I would have to live with the knowledge that nothing is permanent and that I have far less control over my destiny than I knew. My life would never feel the same as it did before the diagnosis. But I learned that it would transform into something more joyful and self-assured as I let go of the driving need for control.

The life of a classical musician is rooted in the futile quest for perfection. Our task is to produce every note, word, and rhythm accurately while making a flawless tone and communicating something no one has ever communicated before in a piece that may have been around for hundreds of years. I have spent the better part of my life as a classical singer fighting my own perfectionism and finally coming to understand that the real art only comes when you are willing to be something other than perfect. The singer who sings every single note perfectly (whatever that means) often fails to inspire emotion in the listener. Therefore we strive to be as perfect as possible but not so perfect that we will resemble robots. Learning to see the beauty in the flaws has been a goal for my singing as well as for my work in the teaching studio. Artistic beauty is seldom defined solely by accuracy.

I have been a singer all of my life and a voice teacher in various ways for more than half of that time. My work—music, singing, and teaching—has been the center of my life. I have published several books on the role that ego plays in all of these pursuits. My sense of myself has been inextricably linked with music.

Since the day of the diagnosis, my perceptions of myself, of my singing, and of my place in the world have all shifted. I now know that I have a brain tumor, and that there is a strong statistical possibility it will someday bring about the end of my life. I also know at a gut level that someday I am going to die. We all understand intellectually that none of us make it out of here alive. But now I realize the truth of that as it applies specifically to me. I may have come to this realization anyway as a result of being in my forties. Perhaps it is fortunate that I learned this in a concrete, indisputable way rather than by developing a creeping dread in mid-life.

I am sure that I am fortunate to have learned about the tumor in time to treat it effectively, and doubly fortunate to live within walking distance of a Harvard Medical School teaching hospital. My priest, Father Sammy Wood, said that I made my trip to the hospital because God Himself put His finger on me and said, "Lynn, *now*." Many of my non-religious friends agreed and speculated that this might be why I made the move to Boston from Denton, Texas just seventeen months earlier.

In the beginning I was confused by the reactions and advice of people in my life. Some said that I was spared because I must have something important left to do. Others said it was clearly not my time. It's easy for me to believe that there's no other rational explanation for the way I learned about the tumor. Even the doctors kept telling me I was the luckiest person they knew. But is there something I'm supposed to do? Even more, is there something I'm supposed to change, something I'm supposed to do *better*?

My priest assured me that there is no biblical basis for that line of thinking. Nowhere in the Bible does God give someone an illness and then spare them from death in order to do something or turn away from something. I found this comforting in that it took the burdens of blame and required action out of the picture during a very complex emotional time.

I do not feel there is something special or important that I was spared to do. I simply don't have those illusions of grandeur about myself or the significance of my life in the large scale of things. But I do feel that in response to the extra time I have been given, I need to consider how I spend it. I know I am one of many who react this way to a diagnosis or a near-death event. I also know that I want to be in service to something larger than myself.

As a Christian, I believe that I am saved through faith and the grace of God, not through my actions. But in response to God's grace, I must live my life with service and love towards others. It's not always easy, and I fail on a daily basis. But still I try, which is what I must continue to do in this second part of my life. During the first year following my diagnosis, I turned often to my faith for strength, and I found it there. Perhaps this was a true epiphany. I didn't understand at the time how much I would need my faith in the coming years, for reasons I could not have anticipated.

This is a book about how my life became infinitely more beautiful after the brain tumor diagnosis. I needed to write about what happened because that is one way I reach understanding of myself and of the world around me. Reading is the other way I find insight. When I scoured the library and the internet for memoirs written by brain tumor survivors, I mostly found memoirs penned by loved ones who had lost someone to a more vicious type of tumor than the one I have. There are also a few memoirs written by people who experienced benign tumors, sometimes coupled with personality changes. My own tumor is a mid-level tumor; not immediately fatal but not exactly non-cancerous. It would have helped me to read about a survivor's experience of one of these mid-level tumors.

My experience is my own, and everyone who receives a diagnosis like this experiences it through their own life and heart. If one person diagnosed with a mid-level tumor finds something to relate to in my story, this book was worth the effort. As I write this today, I reach up to touch the scar on the left side of my head. I imagine it filled with gold-dusted lacquer, holding me together and making me lovelier than I was before the surgery.

—1—
EPIPHANY

Epiphany
noun epiph·a·ny \ i- pi-f -n \
plural: epiphanies
Definition of *Epiphany*
1. *capitalized***:** January 6 observed as a church festival in commemoration of the coming of the <u>Magi</u> as the first manifestation of Christ to the Gentiles or in the Eastern Church in commemoration of the baptism of Christ
2. an appearance or manifestation especially of a divine being
3. a (1). a usually sudden manifestation or perception of the <u>essential</u> nature or meaning of something; **(2).** an intuitive grasp of reality through something (such as an event) usually simple and striking; **(3).** an illuminating discovery, realization, or disclosure
   b: a revealing scene or moment

"We found an abnormality on your brain MRI," Dr. Simon said evenly, leading the group of residents standing around my bedside. "Do you have any family members who can be here today?"

By this time, I had been in the hospital for several days without any idea what was actually wrong. Dr. Simon's words were the beginning of my epiphany. Suddenly I saw my life in a completely new way, but it would be quite some time before illumination or clarity arrived.

On January 5, 2014, around 11:00 PM, I called my friends Ian Mackey and Stephen Eisele (more about them later) and asked them to take me to the emergency room. I had intense pain in the back of my neck, a pain that was familiar to me. While I was in my first summer teaching at the Up North Vocal Institute (2011), I went to the emergency room in Petoskey, Michigan, where the doctor told me I had torticollis (twisted neck), most likely from overuse of my computer. During the 2013 Christmas break, I had spent quite a bit of time on my laptop reviewing pre-screening auditions for the Boston University School of Music, where I was in my first year as chair of the voice department. Since the Michigan doctor had given me painkillers and sent me home, that's what I thought would happen this time. Because it was late on a Sunday night, I tried to wait until the next morning when I could call my primary care physician, but the pain was too intense. And something, some instinct, told me I really needed to go to the emergency room *right now.*

My apartment is located between Boston University and the Fenway, just minutes from the renowned Longwood Medical Area in Boston. The area is home to Brigham and Women's Hospital, Boston Children's Hospital, the Dana Farber Cancer Institute, and Harvard Medical School, among other well-known medical institutions. Ian and Stephen arrived as quickly as possible and asked which hospital I wanted to go to but I was in so much pain I hadn't thought to pick one. I thought we would just go to the closest one. It was late at night and there were a lot of signs for emergency rooms. When we turned into one of the driveways, I thought we had picked Brigham and Women's. As it turned out, this journey began at Beth Israel Deaconess Medical Center on Brookline Ave. Ironically "do you know where you are?" was the first neurological test I was given as well as the only one I failed that night. The nurse gave me a pass since my faculties were otherwise intact. I was crying from the pain (and a little bit of fear and anxiety) but I was definitely not compromised in any obvious neurological way.

Because I also complained of some stomach discomfort and I had a fever, the doctors initially thought I might have meningitis. I spent most of the night on a cot in a secluded area of the emergency room until they eventually took me to an isolation room. Early on January 6 (the Christian feast of the Epiphany), they performed a spinal tap. Many people have since told me these are very painful and have sympathized that I endured one. I hardly remember the experience, perhaps because of everything else that happened afterward, but more likely because I was so tired and in so much pain already from my neck and stomach that the prick in my back barely registered.

The spinal tap was negative, so I was taken for a CT (computerized axial tomography) scan of my head. The CT showed something on my left frontal lobe that looked like a possible stroke, but the ER doctors immediately ruled that out because I had no other stroke symptoms. They decided to admit me to the Neurology service. I sat on a gurney in the hallway for about three hours that afternoon waiting for a bed in Neuro. I remember desperately wishing for some privacy. I felt so exposed lying there in the hallway wearing nothing but a hospital gown and with nothing to do but stare at my rapidly draining iPhone. At some point I became terribly hungry, and my friend Ian was able to score me a turkey sandwich from the nurses before he left to attend our church's Epiphany service.

Early in the evening they moved me into a private room because they still thought I might be highly contagious. I don't remember whether or not I ever had dinner. During the middle of the night I heard a male tech nurse (Matt) saying, "Come here, Johnny." I told him my name was Lynn. He laughed and explained that hospital gowns are commonly referred to as "Johnnies." He couldn't tell me why. Because I have called my brother "Johnny" since we were children, I found the term oddly comforting. Matt dressed me in a fresh Johnny and told me I was being taken for an MRI (magnetic resonance imaging).

I will never forget the way the room looked to me that first time in the MRI machine. The fluorescent lights were white and clear and the machine itself was making a very loud, rhythmic sucking noise. The pictures of palm trees and beaches overhead did nothing to calm my exhausted and panicked state. I gave the MRI technician my glasses and asked if it was OK to sleep during the scan. He laughed and said, "If you can sleep with all that noise, go for it." I tried to close my eyes before they rolled me into the machine so that I wouldn't think about how close a space it was (or wonder what they were looking for). On television hospital dramas, the person in the machine always seems to be moving his or her head around freely, which makes me laugh because in reality, you are packed in so tightly by the helmet and the towels around it that your head is the one thing you can't possibly move. The scan seemed to go on forever in ever-changing patterns of clanging magnets, but I know now that it lasted about forty-five minutes. They must not have used serious ear protection that first time because my ears rang for days afterward, adding to my anxiety about the whole situation.

Early the next morning, I awoke when the neurology team, an attending physician, and eight or nine residents came into my room and stood in a circle around my bed.

"We found an abnormality on your brain scan," said the attending, Dr. Simon. "Do you live alone?" I confirmed that I did.

"Do you have any family that can be here this afternoon?" he asked.

"Could you be a bit more specific about the abnormality?" I asked, trying not to panic immediately. The younger residents were clearly trying to hold back emotion, and I tried not to read anything into that either.

Dr. Simon told me they weren't sure what it was but the best way to describe it was a "lesion." As they showed me the scan, they pointed out that although it covered a large area, it was very thin and close to the surface, so the surgeon would not have to cut through any healthy tissue in order to remove it. They showed me the image: it was a large purple-ish stain that seemed to cover an incredibly large portion of my head. This was the only time I ever saw the image but of course I will never forget what it looked like.

I sat in shocked silence for a few moments, and then they began a long series of neurological tests, all of which I passed. On that first day, there were language tests as well as physical ones—poems I had to read aloud, listing words that started with a particular letter, etc. The doctors quickly established that I had not experienced any loss of language or speech. This was particularly important because the lesion was located on my left frontal lobe, which is the center for language. I told them that I am a voice teacher and singer by profession, so this had special meaning for me. Dr. Simon said he was tempted to ask me to sing but would refrain from doing so.

In the coming days, I was only asked to repeat the language tests for the benefit of the medical students they brought in, while Dr. Simon asked, "Look at her scan. Now listen to her speak. What is your diagnosis?" All of my career experience with authoritarian conductors prepared me well for this particular version of my role as trained seal. In the years following the diagnosis, I became well-versed in the basic physical neurology tests, which focus on balance, peripheral vision, and reflexes.

Dr. Simon was pleased with my performance on the exams. There was every reason to hope for the best, he told me that morning, and I was a "very lucky woman" because of the way they found this tumor. I was sitting on the bed with very little comprehension or absorption of what he was saying. It seemed to happen very fast, and before I knew it, the team of doctors was gone. They seemed to want to give me a little time to digest the news and to call a family member. As they left, they told me that someone from the neurosurgery department would be in to speak with me soon. "Neurosurgery? What?" I thought.

I called my brother John, who lives about ninety minutes away in Rhode Island, and told him what I had learned. It was about 9:30 in the morning. John said he was planning to leave work after lunch even before I called, because at this point I had been in the hospital for two nights already without a diagnosis. He asked if I wanted him to come earlier but I said no. We didn't have any way to know when the neurosurgery people would appear, and it looked like I wouldn't be leaving the hospital any time soon in any event. Twenty minutes later John called back to say he had spoken to his boss and was leaving right now. This will always be one of my fondest memories of my brother.

Alone in the room, I moved to the chair by the window. I spent quite a lot of my hospital time in that chair, staring out at the snow and at the people in cars leading normal lives, and trying to wrap my mind around what was happening. How quickly your life can turn, I thought. Just two days ago I was going about my business, not feeling very well, true, but never thinking anything like this could happen. The indignity of being in the hospital did not help my outlook. I was wearing some clothes (underwear and yoga pants, but no bra or regular shirt were permitted under the Johnny) and I had some books, thanks to Ian and Stephen. But it was hardly a place for a fiercely independent woman like me to feel comfortable.

After a short while the Neurosurgery resident, Dr. C., came in to speak with me. He immediately started educating me about the surgery I would be having for my brain tumor.

"The neurology team said it was a lesion," I said.

"That's what a lesion is: a low-grade brain tumor. It's not our fault that you were admitted to the wrong service," Dr. C. said dismissively. This concept of having two different services (departments) fighting for supremacy over my care was not completely foreign to me. As a career academic, I am familiar with institutional power struggles, and Beth Israel Deaconess Medical Center is a teaching hospital with similar structures in place. Since I was a patient who had just been informed that I had a brain tumor, however, I didn't care much about academic pissing matches.

Dr. C. began his own battery of neurological tests, clucking disapprovingly any time I faltered.

"You are a very anxious person," he said.

"You've just told me I have a low-grade brain tumor," I retorted. "Wouldn't you say anxiety is a normal response?"

The next time I hesitated to answer right away, he said, "You should be confident about your answer."

"Your students must hate you," I couldn't help blurting out.

"I'm sure you have students like this who are weak," he said, completely unfazed. "They must learn to answer with confidence." This made me feel lucky to have studied music instead of a life-and-death pursuit like neurosurgery. Singers and voice teachers need healthy egos in order to succeed; I have written extensively about this. But what kind of ego is required for someone to operate on another person's brain? Dr. Keith Black talks about this in his book *Brain Surgeon: A Doctor's Inspiring Encounters with Mortality and Miracles*. Dr. Black compares neurosurgeons with airline pilots, and says, not surprisingly, that one difficulty of being a neurosurgeon is that line between ego and confidence is too easily crossed. A good neurosurgeon can't be either too nervous or too cocky.

After Dr. C.'s visit, I was quite a bit more rattled. Fortunately, my next guest was Father Sammy from The Church of the Advent (my home church on Beacon Hill). He brought his traveling communion kit and we said the prayers together. This was the first of many times I would experience communion-on-the-go with Father Sammy. I was grateful for the spiritual anchor his visit gave me, and I felt fortified to continue the day's festivities.

When my brother John arrived, I told him I had learned that this was a low-grade brain tumor. His eyes teared up for a moment before his calm, engineer self prevailed. John stayed until late in the evening, and later in the day we were joined by Ian and Stephen. There wasn't much to do but wait for further instructions and try not to bounce off the walls emotionally. Everyone tried to keep the mood light.

At one point I asked the nurse for some Tylenol. She said it had been too soon since my last dose, but she could give me some Oxycontin. I passed on that and then my brother joked, "If she doesn't want it, can I have it?"

One high point of the first afternoon was the visit of Dr. Christopher Stephen, one of the neurology residents. He wanted to speak with me singer-to-singer. He told me he was a choral scholar at the highly regarded Kings College at Cambridge University in England before he became a doctor.

"So you really read music," I teased.

"Oh yes," he said proudly, and proceeded to tell me about some of the famous singers who had performed solos during his time there (John Shirley-Quirk and Jonas Kaufmann, among others. His mellifluous Scottish accent made it easy to believe that he had been a lovely singer (on the tenor II part). Dr. Stephen clearly identified with me on a personal level. He understood who I was and saw me as a respected professional, not just as a patient. This was critically important for me, especially as things unfolded over the next few days.

Late that evening, not long after John, Ian, and Stephen left for the night, I was visited by the surgery team (my third service). Earlier that evening I had undergone a full body scan to make sure the brain tumor wasn't a cancer that had metastasized from a tumor somewhere else in my body. One of the Pieces of Information I Never Thought I'd Need was the knowledge that brain tumors don't spread to other parts of the body. Tumors only metastasize in the other direction: to the brain. The good news from the surgery team was that there weren't any other tumors. The bad news was that I had perforated my colon and I would need surgery for this as soon as possible. This news sent me over the edge.

Throughout the night, my third in the hospital, the nurses woke me every two hours to take vital signs, and various surgical residents came to examine me again and talk to me about the surgery. By the time I was awakened for good at 7:00 by the surgery team and told they were "pulling my food" in anticipation of a late-morning operation, I was exhausted, starved, and emotionally fried. For some reason I was fixated on handling the brain tumor first, probably still operating under the illusion that all of this was going to be resolved quickly. The doctors repeatedly told me that I could die from the perforation and this surgery was non-negotiable.

Dr. Stephen's advice was always the same: I should listen to what my doctors wanted to do. When he came in with the neurology team that morning, he said, "Well, we weren't expecting this." Apparently most people with a perforated colon are in much worse shape than I was. I told them I always feel this bad—I have had gastrointestinal issues since I was a child, frequently related to stress. The fact that I didn't know how bad this issue was would become important in the coming years. But for the moment everything concerning my brain tumor was tabled while the three teams tried to agree on what to do about the perforation.

Finally at midday the surgical attending doctor made the decision to treat my condition with intravenous antibiotics. The surgical resident who had been so confident about my need for surgery now hovered sheepishly in the back of the group. It still took hours for the day nurse to agree to let me eat because she needed the official paperwork. I never realized how difficult a person I would become without food for just half a day. Somehow the intense hunger felt like the last straw, and I was desperate to control something about my personal state.

During the afternoon I was visited by Dr. Alterman, Chief of Neurosurgery, who would perform my surgery himself. Wearing a white coat practically down to his ankles, he was trailed by a group of awestruck residents. "I don't have time to do your surgery this week and they have to take care of this other thing first anyway, since it's the more emergent condition," he said. The idea that my brain tumor was not actually the worst thing I had was hard to fathom.

Dr. Alterman explained that my tumor was flat, like a pancake, and located just under the skull on the left frontal lobe, which was the center for speech and language (which I already knew). I smiled darkly and asked if he knew what I did for a living. When I told him I was a singer and voice professor, he perked up.

"I've actually had patients who weren't able to speak but were able to sing. It's fascinating."

"I'll have quite a time trying to teach voice if I can't speak."

"You won't have to worry about that," he said gently.

After the surgeon and his entourage left, a medical student who had been waiting outside my room came in to interview me for a class paper. My case was apparently considered quite interesting and this student wanted to ask me some questions about how my symptoms had led me to come to the hospital. I asked him if he was excited about wearing the doctor's white coat with "Harvard Medical School" embroidered on it. He said yes, but then he lamented about how short his coat was.

"The nurses know not to ask me anything," he said mournfully. And then, with genuine awe, he asked, "Did you see how long Dr. Alterman's coat was? It's practically to the floor!"

I still find myself noticing the length of the doctors' coats whenever I'm visiting the hospital. It's actually a really ingenious way to signify quickly the doctor's level of skill and knowledge.

That night, my fourth in the hospital, was a tough one. The IV antibiotics made me very ill and I was unable to keep any food down or get any sleep. I felt completely inhuman. One of the night nurses was a beautifully appointed Jamaican woman, with flawless make-up and hair and dressed in a tunic with a cheerful print. I commented on how nice she looked and asked her not to think too badly of the mess I was.

She smiled and said, "Don't worry. When you get out of jail, you will put it all back together."

By Thursday morning I was desperate to leave the hospital, but I knew I was still too ill. Dr. Simon and Dr. Stephen came to speak with me about my options. I was having a functional MRI that day, and if I stayed, I would learn the results sooner. There was also an insurance benefit to having this MRI done while I was still had inpatient status.

Dr. Simon finally said, "You're torn so I'll push: why don't you stay and let us take care of you another night?" They said they would remove the IV at night so I could sleep. And best of all, they said I could take a shower. Fortunately my friend Allison was willing to go to my apartment and bring me some shampoo and other items I needed.

The residents came back to prepare me for the functional MRI. As the website "neuroscientifically challenged" defines it, the functional MRI (fMRI) uses magnetic resonance imaging (MRI) technology to detect changes in cerebral blood flow. When blood flow to a particular brain region is increased, it suggests brain activity in this area has increased. Thus, an fMRI can allow investigators to see what areas of the brain are active when an individual engages in a particular task.

One of the residents said he would give me a little Ativan for anxiety. Dr. Stephen argued protectively, "She needs to be able to perform the tasks." They compromised on a low dosage. As the tech put in my IV for the contrast injection, I asked him for strong ear protection because I have perfect pitch.

"What do you use that perfect pitch for?"

"I'm a voice professor at Boston University."

"Do you know Peter Sykes?" Peter is an organist and the chair of our Historical Performance department and his office is down the hall from mine. "Tell him Mike from choir says hi."

As it turned out, Mike sings in the choir at Peter's church. I found that small connection so comforting. In numerous future visits to the MRI lab "Mike from choir" would advocate for me when I insisted on better ear protection than the tiny ear plugs.

During the functional MRI, Mike gave me instructions for each section: say all of the words you can think of that start with the letter "P," or tap your right foot for the next ten seconds, etc. The test was designed to record which parts of my brain were associated with different capabilities. Dr. Alterman would not be able to remove the entire tumor because it had "fingers" in my brain and I needed to be able to function after the surgery. The tumor's remaining fingers, of course, would be monitored for the rest of my life. This fMRI would help him determine just how much he could safely remove. I would have found this exam incredibly interesting if it had been happening to someone other than me.

Five days into my stay, I was finally able to eat breakfast, and that meant I was given clearance to leave. Most importantly, the functional MRI showed no change at all in the tumor over the past few days, which strengthened their hypothesis that this was likely not a fast-growing, cancerous tumor. Without a biopsy, of course, there was no way to be sure or to estimate any kind of prognosis. They gave me a prescription for an oral version of the IV antibiotic I had been taking for the colon perforation.

The other residents laughed when Dr. Stephen said that if I drank alcohol while taking these, I would wish I had never been born. He didn't laugh. "I'm serious. Not one drop."

Dr. Simon wished me well and apologized again that they hadn't paid more attention to my stomach pain at the beginning. (This is how diligent the doctors are at Beth Israel. They found a brain tumor and a perforated colon when I came in for an unrelated neck spasm, and they were apologizing for not diagnosing both conditions even sooner than two days.) I told him how grateful I was for everything they had found and for the excellent care I received.

Back at home, I was in limbo for the next few days. I received many calls from the hospital explaining how to prepare for my brain surgery, formally known as a craniotomy: the surgical body wash I would need to use, when to stop eating, and how early I should arrive on the actual morning. I spent a lot of time starting out the window and talking with friends and family on the phone. John and his wife Beth brought the kids up to Boston for a day visit with me. I had lost some weight during the week but no one laughed when I joked that I was "just one brain tumor away from my ideal weight" (a reference to Emily Blunt's character's comment about stomach flu in the movie *The Devil Wears Prada*).

The first day of the spring semester at BU was January 15. I didn't see any reason not to teach lessons that day and wanted to avoid sitting around all day thinking about the surgery. So I went to school as usual. My students, of course, had no idea what was happening because they were on the holiday break when I spent five days in the hospital. The official party line for the coming days was that I was having some tests done. I knew my students would raise an eyebrow at this. It was completely unlike me to miss any time at the beginning of the semester just for tests, particularly when we had just had a month-long break. I couldn't worry about that yet, though, and I deflected any questions from them that day.

On the morning of January 16, I tried to be calm. My brother had a work trip to Manhattan that day and was unable to get out of it, so my friend Allison picked me up bright and early to drive me to the hospital. When I arrived, they did another MRI just to see exactly where things stood. The tech who put in the IV told me I'd be up and around before I knew it, because brain surgery is a surprisingly easy recovery. After the MRI, Allison was still waiting and insisted on waiting there a while longer. I was grateful for her presence even though I felt guilty that she had to stay.

They took me to the pre-op area and showed me the consent form. When I saw all of the possible outcomes (paralysis, incapacitation, and death, among other attractive options), I began to panic. Then one of the nurses said I should go ahead and shave my whole head right now "just to save time for when the treatment starts." "I have a performance in six weeks, I can't do that!" I shouted. My denial of my situation was in full bloom.

Dr. Alterman came in and said he would do his best to preserve my hair but there were "more important things for him to consider." Then he turned to the anesthesiologist and told her to give me some Ativan. They also went to get Allison to come sit with me. She was amazing; she sat close to my head and kept saying calming things. The last thing I remember was being on the table in the operating room and watching them take off my underwear. I wondered what they were going to do with it, and whether or not I would get it back.

When I woke up in the ICU, Dr. Alterman was asking me questions: "Do you know your name? Do you know where you are?"

I answered everything correctly and everyone around the bed looked visibly relieved. Having later read about many more cases, I now know how risky brain surgery is, and how that first moment tells the surgeon whether or not the surgery has "wrecked" the patient. My surgery had lasted almost four hours. Dr. Alterman said all had gone well and he would call my brother to let him know.

During the day my head hurt quite a bit but they kept me heavily medicated. In the afternoon they wheeled me away for a CT scan. The nurses were not terribly gentle and they asked me to move myself from the gurney into the machine, which was incredibly painful. When it was time for dinner, I was hungry. But then I spontaneously threw up all over my dinner tray without any physical warning. I cried with embarrassment.

It was an eerie night in the ICU. The alarm on my monitor kept going off, and each time it did the nurses would wake me and tell me to breathe. Apparently the machine was set to let them know if I stopped breathing or if my respiration rate sank too low. I was very glad to see the light of the next day and eager to see my brother John. The day nurse Tanya [not her real name] made the day bearable for both me and my brother. I found it horribly degrading to have someone help me relieve myself. I am a fiercely independent person and I cried each and every time. But Tanya helped me to understand that this was necessary and she never made me feel ashamed. I am so grateful for the skills of the stellar doctors who have managed my conditions but I owe my sanity during my hospital stays to these exemplary nurses, the ones who treated me as an actual person and provided whatever comfort was permitted.

Of course John was a godsend as well. He brought me lunch from Subway so I wouldn't have to eat the hospital food, and he explained everything to my mother and sister on the phone. I found it too upsetting to speak with them at first. Part of me wanted to take care of their feelings about this but part of me knew I needed to focus on getting through it myself. My brother was mostly just present in the room, making jokes and handling the scientific information we were getting from the doctors. He's an engineer, not a "feelings" person. My mother and sister are both educators like me, deeply empathetic people, and John's rationality just happened to be what I needed at the time.

I was seen that day by two doctors who would be part of my treatment after the diagnosis was made. The radiation specialist scared me half to death by going into elaborate detail about the radiation I would be having. I didn't even have a diagnosis yet—it would be another ten days before I got the biopsy results—and I had no mental compartment for the information he was overloading me with. At that stage, I still understood the diagnosis options as binary: either the tumor would be benign and I would walk away scot-free, or it would be malignant and I would never go back to work. The days and months ahead would prove the assessment to be much less clear than that.

I was also visited for the first time by Dr. Uhlmann, my neuro-oncologist. Dr. Uhlmann is Hungarian, very tall, and very serious at all times. It became my mission to get him to crack a smile, in part because I was so thoroughly frightened by the situation and also because I was desperate to put things on a more quotidian level. Dr. Uhlmann mentioned the probability of chemotherapy but somehow his manner was much quieter and less alarming than the radiation doctor's had been.

As he pulled back the foil on my head to take a look at my incision, I joked that I was picking up Russia on this thing. His lips turned up in the tiniest but yet visible way. Still a victory. After he left, John noted with pride that I'd been able to get the serious doctor to smile.

I had yet another MRI that afternoon so they would have a post-surgery baseline for my tumor. As they wheeled in my gurney, I recognized the voice of one of the techs: Mike From Choir. This small familiarity helped me immeasurably. I told Mike that moving me into the CT machine the previous day had been terribly painful.

"You don't have to do anything. You're with MRI now, not CT. You're in a Porsche, not a Ford Terrell," Mike said as four people lifted me off the gurney before I had time to feel any pain.

In the late afternoon they told me I would be moved out of the ICU into a regular room very soon and I would most likely be going home the next day. John waited with me for the hours it took for them to find a bed for me. I was eager to get out of the ICU, but once they moved me I no longer had my own room. I was in the half of the room closest to the window and the bathroom, and there was only space for the bed and the one chair. The other half of the room was occupied by a very old woman who moaned quietly and continuously.

As they were rolling me down the hall toward the new room, I thought I saw Dr. Stephen (the singer-resident) at the end of the hall, and I asked John to go get him. John told me he asked Dr. Stephen if he remembered John's sister the singer and Dr. Stephen said, "She's here?" as he sped down the hall. It was still painful for me to turn my head so he held my hand while he confirmed that they'd done a craniotomy and we didn't have biopsy results yet. He told me he had some things he must do but wished me well. His caring meant so much to me.

The first thing I did in the new room was get up to use the bathroom alone. All kinds of bells and alarms sounded, and within seconds five or six nurses ran into the room. The code ended when they saw that I was fine; they thought I had fallen off the bed. Thankfully they agreed to turn off the bed alarms so I would be allowed to move freely within the room on my own.

I ordered some dinner (plain pasta with butter and parmesan) and said goodbye to John. It was not lost on me that this was Friday night of the MLK holiday weekend, and it was also his wife Beth's last day at her current job. John couldn't have gotten back to his home in Rhode Island before 8:00 or 8:30 that night at the earliest.

During the night I was alone with my thoughts. The nurses took vital signs every two hours, so sleep was impossible. I plugged in my iPhone (the cord just barely reached the bed) so I could listen to calming music and drown out the various hospital sounds. I cued up a playlist I had made called "Mellow Music." I think of that lonely night whenever I hear the haunting Sara Bareilles song "Manhattan." (Later her songs "Brave" and "Chasing the Sun," also from her album *The Blessed Unrest*, would be helpful to my recovering spirit.) My head ached enough that I didn't want to read, and there is *never* a time that I don't want to read, as my close friends know. I asked the nurses for a cold compress to put across my eyes. The night seemed to last for many, many hours.

The next morning a light snow was falling so it took John a little while to get back to Boston. This was now the third day in a row that he was making the trip, ninety minutes each way. We waited in my room for an interminable amount of time but the nurse finally brought the release papers and got Dr. Simon's signature. I asked if I could return to work on Tuesday after the MLK holiday on Monday.

Yes, my level of denial was that high. The nurse laughed and said no, I wasn't going back to work until I was cleared by Dr. Uhlmann at my biopsy results appointment on January 27, nine days away. The only reason they were letting me leave now was that "most people recover more quickly at home." They sent me off with a list of prescriptions to pick up at the nearby CVS store.

John brought his car around and let me out in front of the store to get the prescriptions, as the Longwood area is quite crowded and it was necessary for him to circle the block while I went inside. Minutes later I returned to the car in a panic because I realized I didn't have my debit card; it had been taken from me with my other valuables before the surgery. John gently said it was no problem; I could use his credit card now and he would retrieve mine from the hospital later. After I paid for the scrips, I went to the food court to get us lunch. But I was exhausted, overwhelmed, and uncharacteristically incapable of handling this simple task. I went back to the car where John was double-parked with the hazard lights on. Again he said it was no problem, we'd go home and he would get us food somewhere. Back at home, John went out into my neighborhood to pick up some groceries and some lunch. I felt unable to make even the smallest decision. Before he left, John came into the bathroom with me to remove my surgical bandage.

"Let's see how bad it is," I said.

If he was as freaked out as I was, he didn't show it. We slowly pulled off the bandage to reveal a shaved area about a quarter inch wide which extended from the top of my head down to just in front of the top of my left ear. Weaving down through the shaved area was a braided stitch holding my skull together. The ridge of this area, where my skull eventually braided itself without the thread, will always be there, even though my hair has grown back. Dr. Alterman left a lock of hair in front of the scar so the shaved area was actually fairly easy to conceal, especially after a few weeks. John promised to come back to accompany me to the appointment on January 27, and my wait for the results began.

Nine days stretched out in front of me. Those nine days represent a unique time in my life. I wasn't sure how to think about things at first. On the first day I would have been back in school, the Tuesday after MLK day, I began a practice of reading the Daily Office Lectionary from *The Book of Common Prayer* and copying down verses that moved me, marking certain verses with an asterisk as particularly helpful.

> From my journal entry on January 21, 2014:
> The Lord is my strength and my shield;
> in him, my heart trusts.
> so I am helped, and my heart exults.
> and with my song I give thanks to him.
>
> Psalm 28:7

> Wait and pray. My doctors have much hope that the tumor is not aggressive, and I am doing my very best to go with that. . . . God be with me. Your will, not mine, but I hope it is not yet my time.

I filled the time with many distractions, and many friends came by to help. I had been given an Apple TV for Christmas, so I signed up for Netflix. I started to watch *Breaking Bad* (otherwise known as "the greatest TV show of all time") but when Walt was diagnosed with lung cancer in the first episode, I put that on hold. I ended up binge-watching *The West Wing*—which was incredibly smart, optimistic viewing—and making my way through several novels.

In the early twentieth century, the term "liminality" was coined by Arnold van Gennep and then used by Victor Turner to describe the ambiguity that happens in the middle stage of a rite of passage, when the old self is finished but the new way of life has not yet begun. From the Latin *limen* (on the threshold), "liminal space" is used more broadly now as simply the time between "what was" and "the next." Theologian Richard Rohr goes as far as to say that all transformation takes place in liminal space, and that this is the only way we can grow and find peace.

I spent about three weeks in a clearly liminal space and then months more in something like liminal space. Each morning I awoke and remembered: "I have a brain tumor!" And then I reached for my Bible. It was comforting to find out how strong my faith really was. I started out praying for the tumor to be benign but found myself led to pray for the strength to manage whatever was coming, and with thanksgiving for the excellent doctors and for my family and friends. I was still relatively new to Boston and found that I had a stronger network of new friends than I had thought. I considered my new life in Boston and how badly I wanted to return to it, just as it was. I felt sure that God had put me in Boston to receive the care I needed, or at the very least, to reveal my condition to me while I was in this mecca of American healthcare. The liminal space was a time of enormous peace and growth for me.

I waited and prayed through those days and entertained myself as well as I could, trying to rest and recover so that I could return to work as soon as I knew it was benign. I was, of course, still operating from the premise that the results would be all or nothing. In those early days I didn't have enough information about brain tumors, including how many different kinds there are, to think about this in any other terms. I'm grateful now that I didn't know how many possibilities existed.

At that time I was living with the three cats I brought with me from Texas, Jeoffrey, Fred, and Annie. Jeoffrey and Fred were 10-year-old tuxedo cats from the same litter, and Annie was a cute little black 9-year-old. Every night during that time, Fred slept at my feet and Jeoffrey and Annie slept down either side of me. The only other time Jeoffrey and Annie slept in this formation was the night I came home without my first cat, Emily. On the last night before the biopsy results appointment, the boys slept in the living room and Annie slept with her front paws on my arm. I took this to mean they thought I was fine now.

On the day of the appointment, I wrote in my journal:

Today is the day. God, I believe that you hear my prayers and I believe in your plan for my life. I pray that I will be able to return to the life you have so graciously blessed me with.

> But I am like a green olive tree in the house of God.
> I trust in the steadfast love of God forever and ever.
> I will thank you forever, because of what you have done.
> In the presence of the faithful, I will proclaim your name,
> for it is good.
>
> Psalm 52:8–9

The appointment was scheduled for 4:00 so I had most of the day to wait. I couldn't focus enough to read or watch anything. I just kept trying to breathe and stay positive. John arrived at 3:00 for the drive over to Beth Israel.

It was time to see how bad it was.

—2—

DOCTORS

Many of us looking back through life would say that the kindest man we have ever known has been a medical man, or perhaps that surgeon whose fine tact, directed by deeply informed perception, has come to us in our need with a more sublime beneficence than that of miracle-workers.

GEORGE ELIOT, *MIDDLEMARCH*

We all come in contact with many doctors throughout our lives, most often in routine visits but also in our most frightening moments. In these moments we depend nakedly on their medical expertise and we may find ourselves desperately seeking a personal connection with them as a way to hold off the fear of the unknown. Emily Transue, MD, writes about the chemistry that happens between doctors and patients:

> [It is] so strong in some interactions and so elusive in others . . . doctors and patients, like lovers or friends, can have a deep instinct to connect with each other in some instances and not in others. You can work around the connection, care for someone without it, learn to modulate it; the bond can appear suddenly after a long time of being absent. But that basic connection is real.
>
> from *On Call: A Doctors' Days & Nights in Residency*

I experienced a strong personal connection with Dr. Stephen during my initial hospital stay, and the connection sustained me. Perhaps even more importantly, it made me more inclined to trust what he told me.

As a teacher, I have experienced varying levels of chemistry with my students. Some students bond instantly; our shared personality traits make it feel as though we have always known each other. In other cases, it takes months for the bond to develop, months during which I continually search for common ground and a way to let the student know they can trust me. In rare cases, students who are my polar opposite (usually the free spirit, less type-A personality) never really bond with me. But every now and then, I find myself learning something new about music and about myself when an unlikely bond suddenly happens after a long period of time. It is impossible to predict whether or not we will find common ground.

Dr. Uhlmann, the serious Hungarian neuro-oncologist who would become my guide on this journey, is someone I bonded with over time rather than immediately. I learned to trust his kindness and to appreciate the care he took with his words on every visit. But my first visit to his office to learn the biopsy results was nothing but terrifying. I can't blame him for this, for these circumstances would have frightened most reasonable people.

John and I waited in the office suite, helpfully marked by a large sign outside that read "Brain Tumor Clinic." I tried not to look around at the other patients, many of whom had obvious active symptoms. We made small talk until we were finally summoned inside, where Dr. Uhlmann and Dr. R. (the radiation doctor) were waiting.

I was not prepared for the vagueness of the news we heard that day from the two doctors. They told me they were still waiting for the full results of the biopsy from the lab so they didn't have all of the genetic information they needed in order to decide whether we would do chemotherapy or radiation or some combination of the two. I was confused. We didn't seem to have any kind of diagnosis yet, so how did we know that I would definitely need treatment? Clearly I was still hoping for an all-or-nothing reveal during this appointment, which is just not how brain tumors are diagnosed and treated. They had already told me they couldn't remove the tumor in its entirety, and I should have understood that this appointment had a zero percent chance of being my last one.

"Would you describe the tumor as benign?" I asked after they had been talking for a while.

"Yes," Dr. Uhlmann said, but his voice lifted upward in a way that suggested the opposite, or at least indicated a lack of confidence in the answer.

John asked a lot of questions while I sat there trying not to have a meltdown. I wanted to scream or cry or vomit but instead I just sat still. They explained again that the neurosurgeon had removed most of the tumor, and all of the doctors believed that it was a slow-growing tumor. But the tumor still had fingers in my brain.

"Most people choose to do something about that," said Dr. Uhlmann.

Since they didn't have all of the lab results back yet, I was still recovering from the surgery, and I was scheduled to sing a concert at the beginning of March, the doctors agreed to postpone any treatment decisions until my next appointment on March 10. They were adamant that some kind of treatment would take place after that time. I should have taken comfort in the lack of immediacy but I was too surprised not to have the solid answers I thought I would get that day.

Dr. R. left at that point, and Dr. Uhlmann turned to the removal of my surgical stitches. Once the serious conversation came to a close, John tried to joke with Dr. Uhlmann, who wasn't really having it. Dr. Uhlmann appraised my stitches with considerable awe, calling them "beautiful." He hesitated to take them out without direct instruction from Dr. Alterman but ultimately decided to go ahead. I was grateful for the relief because my head had healed enough that the stitches were pulling at my scalp and causing me headaches. It took some time for him to remove all of them and we talked during the process.

Dr. Uhlmann asked about the concert I was scheduled to do in just about five weeks. "Are you a member of the choir?"

"No, no, she's the soloist down front," John quickly interjected with no small amount of pride, which touched me deeply. I know that my family is proud of my performance career but it's not something we often discuss. It was affirming to know that my brother appreciates what I do.

"May I color my hair?" I then asked.

"If you must," Dr. Uhlmann replied.

We had a lengthy debate about driving. I would be on the anti-seizure medication Keppra for months to come but it would still be possible for me to experience a seizure while taking it. Seizures, after all, are a common symptom of these tumors, and people often learn they have a brain tumor after they have a seizure. I walk to work and only use my car to do errands and to take the occasional trip down to Rhode Island. In the end I received approval to drive short distances, and I was instructed to call immediately if I had any issues. In the state of Massachusetts, having a seizure automatically leads to the loss of your license for at least six months. I hope to avoid ever coming up against that law.

John and I left not knowing how to feel. It wasn't disastrous news but it didn't feel entirely positive either. I was still operating on the all-or-nothing premise, and this appointment didn't point to either one. Since we didn't have all of the results and I was clearly not going to just sail off into the sunset, I felt unsettled. We decided to dine at Audubon Boston before John headed back to RI. While we ate, we tried to convince each other that the news had actually been good. This would be one of the first big life lessons the tumor taught me: how to seek peace in the many gray areas life throws us.

The next morning I arose and prepared to return to school. Being able to do this reminded me that this could all have turned out very differently. I wrote in my journal:

> Thank you, God!!!
>
> Thank you for the gift of returning to my life.
>
> Thank you for the time you are giving me so generously.
>
> Help me to serve the people in my life with love, patience, and gladness.
>
> I am so blessed.

I dressed carefully, choosing a brown cap to hide the shaved scar until I talked with my studio class that evening. A friend gave me a ride to school so I would not have to risk the icy sidewalks of Boston in January. Back in my office I felt like Jimmy Stewart at the end of the movie *It's a Wonderful Life,* when he kisses the broken topper as it comes off the newel of the staircase into his hand. All I dreamed of during my convalescence was returning to my regular life, good and bad rolled up together in one lucky package. It had been just twelve days since my surgery. I didn't yet understand the limbo that was beginning.

Just two days after the results appointment I started to feel an anxiety that I had not faced during the days on my couch. Somehow I couldn't absorb the fact that I didn't have brain cancer (at least, they didn't think I did; the lab results would tell us for sure) and that I wasn't going to die right away. I had held my emotions together for three weeks without letting my mind go to the worst place but now I couldn't seem to find a safe place. I began to have trouble sleeping as I kept worrying about the treatment and about not having any kind of clear prognosis. I also had to get used to the idea that I was forced to ask for, and receive, lots of help, some from places and people I didn't expect. As an independent professional woman who was still new to the city, I was unaccustomed to letting others help me manage my daily life but now I had no choice.

During this time the smallest things seemed large. My first trip to the store by myself, getting up in the morning and feeding my cats, and working with my students: these were things I had always done and taken for granted as things I would always be doing. But as Jane Kenyon notes in one of my favorite poems, someday it will be otherwise. Another key lesson began to emerge: I need to take better care of my own physical and emotional needs. Instead of being on the hamster wheel all the time, trying to achieve as much as possible and please everyone in the process, I could rest when I needed to, ignore email that wasn't urgent, make healthier meals, say no if I'm too tired, and generally try to be less hard on myself than I've been for decades. I battled between fear about the tumor and gratitude for the knowledge about myself that I gained from it, and that battle continues.

Now that I'm farther away from that tender time, I understand that these feelings are hardly unique to me. In Paul Kalanithi's luminous book about his terminal cancer, *when breath becomes air*, he describes how he felt after the initial shock of the diagnosis and flurry of activity around it:

> It struck me that I had traversed the five stages of grief . . . but I had done it all backwards. On diagnosis, I'd been prepared for death. I'd even felt good about it. I'd accepted it. I'd been ready. Then I slumped into a depression, as it became clear that I might not be dying so soon after all, which is, of course, good news, but also confusing and strangely enervating. (p. 161)

I was back in my life but had no real picture of how things were going to play out. It was another odd period of limbo from January 27 until March 10, when I would know more. I taught, I sang, I prayed, and I felt sad and scared a lot of the time. I was not seeing a therapist at the time and I'm sure I was difficult to be with around family and friends. At night I read piles of novels and tried to hide. And as Hillary Clinton put it in her book about the 2016 election, wine helped too.

My faith turned out to be stronger than I realized, and it was the life jacket I clung to most firmly, especially in the darkest moments. I was reading the Daily Office every morning and feeling comfort in so many of the verses I read. In early February, the gift of a snow day came just when I needed it the most. It had been three weeks since the surgery and I was still far from my normal self. I found strength in the book of Hebrews:

> Endure trials for the sake of discipline. God is treating you
> as children; for what child is there whom a parent does
> not discipline?
>
> Therefore lift your drooping hands and strengthen your
> weak knees, and make straight paths for your feet, so
> that what is lame may not be put out of joint, but rather
> be healed. Pursue peace with everyone, and the holiness
> without which no one will see the Lord.
>
> Hebrews 12:7, 12–14

There is always a way forward, even if it feels like I can't keep going.

In addition to the Daily Office, I also used the devotional guide *Power Thoughts*, which I had bought on a whim just days before I went into the hospital. I am skeptical of the so-called prosperity gospel (God wants me to be wealthy) or the idea that Christians should be happy in order to invite happiness into their lives. But Joyce Meyer's vocabulary of fighting for a positive attitude and taking care of the self resonated strongly with me during this time. On one day when I was feeling guilty about canceling my studio class in order to shorten a twelve-hour day, I read this combination of thoughts:

> Martha, Martha, you are worried and distracted by many
> things; there is need of only one thing.
>
> Luke 10: 41-42
>
> Power Thought: I have balance in my life. I enjoy
> my work, and I know when to stop and enjoy
> other things.

The next day there was an entry about surprise, which also resonated loudly with me:

> Beloved, do not be surprised at the fiery ordeal that is taking place among you to test you, as though something strange were happening to you. But rejoice insofar as you are sharing Christ's sufferings, so that you may also be glad and shout for joy when his glory is revealed.
>
> 1 Peter 4:12–13

I wrote in my journal that day, "This experience has definitely been a test for me, a surprise of epic proportions. Am I passing the test?" I felt a constant need to integrate this surprise into my vision for my life, and to understand what its place in my thinking should be. I knew I needed to build up the strength to endure treatment, and I questioned my approach to the situation on an almost daily basis. I also struggled with guilt whenever I needed to take time to rest, which added to my unsettled feelings about my situation.

After I was released from the hospital, I sent a letter to Dr. Stephen through his BIDMC residency program. I wanted to thank him in writing for his kindness towards me, and to offer him a pair of tickets to my upcoming concert. (I also offered tickets to Dr. Alterman and Dr. Uhlmann, both of whom politely declined.) During the week before the concert, I was thrilled to receive a phone call from Dr. Stephen.

Addressing me as "Professor," he thanked me for my letter and asked how I was doing. I knew that he really wanted to know, which brought tears to my eyes. I began to tell him that I was back at work, that I got tired from time to time, but then I realized he probably didn't know anything about my test results. I told him the tumor was essentially benign and he loudly exhaled and said they'd been pretty confident that it was. He said it was something I'd always have to monitor. I told him they were recommending further treatment but I was leaning towards watching and waiting because treatment seems invasive and would definitely affect my quality of life.

Dr. Stephen again emphasized that I should be sure to listen to the advice of my neuro-oncologist, and asked who they'd given me. When I told him, he laughed enthusiastically.

"Dr. Uhlmann is a very kind man. And he knows his stuff," he said.

"This has changed my life," I said.

"Of course it has," he answered. "And it probably adds emotional depth to your singing."

He thanked me profusely for the letter and said he doesn't often hear from patients, even less so here in the States. He told me he respects that I'm the head of voice at such a prestigious institution. He gladly accepted the offer of tickets for him and his wife for my concert. They did attend, and he sent me a lovely email afterward.

Speaking with Dr. Stephen put me at ease heading into my next appointment with Dr. Uhlmann. Dr. Stephen's earnest manner was so calming and reassuring, and I was buoyed by his obvious respect and approval of Dr. Uhlmann as a fortunate assignment for me. Dr. Stephen's care for me and for my situation extended beyond his duties as a resident, and I will always think of him as an angel on earth.

Following my concert performance, the date of my next appointment arrived on March 10, and with it my bond with Dr. Uhlmann began to strengthen. This time it was just the two of us;

it had been determined that radiation would not be our course, so I never saw Dr. R. again. I'm sure he has many lovely qualities but his blunt, overly jargonistic way of presenting my options was absolutely terrifying. I attended the appointment alone, as I couldn't keep asking my brother to drive up to Boston to accompany me every time when there was no clear end in sight. Dr. Uhlmann had the pathology report and was ready to give me more definitive information now.

From the final surgical pathology report, the pathological diagnosis:

Brain, left, resection
  –Oligodendroglioma, WHO grade II of IV, see note.
  –Co-deletion for 1p and 19q detected by FISH.

Note: The tumor is mildly to moderately hypercellular and has an oligodendroglial phenotype. There is focal moderate nuclear pleomorphism and there are few mitoses. There is no evidence of necrosis or vascular proliferation in the specimen examined. However, given the presence of mitosis and slight increase and nuclear pleomorphism and proliferative activity, a closer follow-up is recommended.

I understood almost nothing of the report. Dr. Uhlmann explained that level II tumors of this kind are a gray area in the medical literature. Level I tumors are treated with "watch and wait" while level III and IV tumors require immediate care, but the medical profession has not reached consensus on how to treat level II tumors. Some doctors treat level II as level I and do nothing while others treat it as a level III (high-grade) tumor, which is what he planned to do. My tumor might turn out to be nothing going forward, or it might come back later as a level III. There is no way to predict which outcome will occur.

The good news here was that I had positive results on the 1p/19q chromosome test. This means that the tip is missing in the tumor cells, which means in turn that these tumor cells are sensitive to chemotherapy. From the report:

> In oligodendroglioma, co-deletion of 1p/19q has been associated with excellent response to chemotherapy and long survival.

Dr. Uhlmann recommended pill chemotherapy (temozolomide) for twelve months, with MRIs every two months and blood work once a week. I would take the pill for five days each month with twenty-three days off until the next cycle.

I was terribly reluctant to do the chemotherapy, somehow still hoping that I had a choice. I harbored a delusion that I could just walk away from this and resume my normal life if we decided to watch and wait. Dr. Uhlmann sat with me for about forty-five minutes, answering all of my questions and patiently guiding me to the plan he knew was the right one. He told me I would feel somewhat nauseous on the pill days but I would most likely not experience vomiting and I would definitely not lose my hair. As someone who was relatively young and healthy, I would probably sail through without any real issues, he said, and we could always stop if I was unable to tolerate the pills. He was adamant that I should not wait until the end of the semester to begin, for the longer I waited, the more could happen. We would be doing this treatment to ensure that the tumor's fingers in my brain wouldn't have a chance to upgrade themselves.

Ultimately Dr. Ulhmann argued that my fear about the chemotherapy treatment should not outweigh the fear that five to ten years from now this tumor could turn into a level III. I could see no way around that rationale. Dr. Uhlmann emphasized that I was young and healthy and he wanted to "keep me that way." I could see his genuine caring for me and for my thought process and feelings during this lengthy conversation. By the time I left his office, I was uneasy about starting the chemotherapy but I knew I had a strong, highly competent ally in this fight, and I trusted him with my life. Without that trust and the personal connection I had with my doctor, I would have suffered far more intensely than I did over the coming months.

A few days after that appointment I experienced the opposite of compassionate care when I went to see my primary care doctor to arrange for the blood work I would be having every week. This would be the last time I'd see Dr. C., who retired not long afterward. But he etched a permanent place in my story with his performance during my final visit to his office.

After reading the pathology report, Dr. C. excused himself to go look up oligodendroglioma, with which he was unfamiliar. When he returned, he told me that the good news is that I have the chromosome, and I should be glad because my "ten-year survival chances look really good."

If he said other things to me that day, I didn't hear them. Ten years! I wouldn't even be sixty yet. I had not been thinking about this tumor as inevitably terminal. Dr. Uhlmann had never given me any kind of prognosis or statistical probability and all of my doctors had advised me to stay off the Internet.

I went into a major tailspin after Dr. C. casually congratulated me on the likelihood that I would still be alive in ten years. I started searching the Internet for confirmation and quickly found multiple sources that said the median survival rate for a grade II oligo is eleven years. It didn't seem to be a question of "if" it would upgrade but rather "when." BU was out for spring break so I had far too much time to read of all the sad oligo stories I could find. One day I tried to distract myself by visiting the special Impressionist exhibit at the Museum of Fine Arts, where I am a member. I found myself checking the birth and death dates, calculating each person's time on earth, and thinking, "These people are all dead." I went upstairs to the contemporary section where the death dates were all open. That's how dark things were for a while.

Years later when I read Paul Kalanithi's book, I saw that he understood this darkness far better than Dr. C. had:

> The reason doctors don't give patients specific prognoses is not merely because they cannot... What patients seek is not scientific knowledge that doctors hide but existential authenticity each person must find on her own. Getting too deeply into statistics is like trying to quench a thirst with salty water. The angst of facing mortality has no remedy in probability.

Dr. C.'s flippant treatment of my situation was insensitive, to be sure, but chances are good that I would have experienced the breakdown of facing my own mortality regardless. Eventually I would have come across these numbers myself. He just ensured that the timing coincided with the onset of chemotherapy.

The chemo itself was not as bad as I expected. I felt tired and vaguely nauseous, especially by the fourth and fifth days, but I didn't lose my hair or actually become sick. I prayed each night as I forced the pills down and tried to think about them as healing to me, not as poison. I can see the toxic effect of the treatment in pictures of me from the time in which I look like a lawn that has just been sprayed with pesticide: a bit dead around the edges.

Dealing with the specialty pharmacy that sent me the pills was, unbelievably, the most difficult aspect of the treatment process. There is a special place in hell for the incompetent people I spoke to there on a regular basis. I am an organized, educated person and I found it almost impossible to get the correct pills delivered to the correct address on the correct day. Of all the worries associated with my tumor, this should not have been an additional burden. Their representatives were rude and sloppy. My anger over this was considerable, and it raised my stress to barely tolerable levels.

Each time I started a new pill cycle, usually after receiving the pills at the last possible moment before I was supposed to start, I tried to calm myself. My friend Jennifer advised me to pray over these pills and to see them as God's way of helping me get better, not as a poisonous toxin that would cause me unknown physical distress. Most of the time this helped make it possible to swallow the pills at eleven o'clock each of the five nights. By the time I reached the fifth night, I had major difficulty swallowing them, and managed it only by knowing I would have twenty-three days until the next dose.

I turned again and again to my Bible to get me through these moments. Some of the verses that were particularly soothing to me:

Let the Lord your God show us where we should go and what we should do.... Whether it is good or bad, we will obey the voice of the Lord our God.

Jeremiah 42:3, 6

> And can any of you by worrying add a single hour to your
> life?... So do not worry about tomorrow, for tomorrow will bring
> worries of its own. Today's trouble is enough for today.
>
> Matthew 6:27, 34

> To set the mind on the flesh is death, but to set the mind on
> the Spirit is life and peace.
>
> Romans 8:6

When I read the Gospel story about the apostles who were afraid because waves were coming into their boat, I realized that I often felt like waves were coming in my boat during that winter. But Jesus calmed the wind and the waves and said to them, "Why are you afraid? Have you still no faith?" (Mark 4:40). Reading these verses didn't remove my fear but it did keep the fear from growing so large that it overwhelmed my life. I lived with a lot of uncertainty during the first round of chemo, waiting for my April appointment with Dr. Uhlmann so I could ask him about my "ten-year survival chances" and learn whether or not my tumor had grown.

Just before that appointment my friend Dan told me about Stephen Jay Gould's famous essay, "The Median is Not the Message." Gould, a paleontologist, science writer, and professor at Harvard, was diagnosed with the rare cancer peritoneal mesothelioma at the age of forty. After researching statistics against the advice of his doctors, he learned that the median survival time for his cancer was eight months. But then he posited that half of the patients must live longer than that time. Given the fact that no one lives for zero amount of time from diagnosis, the statistic has to be skewed toward the side of longer life.

Then Gould factored in all of the conditions that would put him on the right side of the statistic: early diagnosis, relative youth, best medical care in the nation (also in Boston), the ability to follow the doctor's instructions, and most importantly, a positive attitude. Statistical averages are merely useful abstractions, he said, and by themselves do not encompass "our actual world of variation, shadings, and continua." (Wikipedia contributors, "Stephen Jay Gould," *Wikipedia, The Free Encyclopedia,* accessed June 14, 2018). In the end, Gould survived his cancer and he died of an unrelated cancer twenty years later at the age of sixty.

It is easy to lose sight of the miracle of modern medicine. We have no idea how fortunate we are to live in a time when new treatments are being developed every day. Recently I read John Gunther's memoir *Death Be Not Proud* about the death of his teenage son, John Gunther, Jr. First published in 1949, this moving tribute highlights how treatments have progressed over the intervening years. Gunther writes of X-ray therapy, mustard gas injections, and the Gerson diet (no salt or fat and multiple enemas), treatments that sound primitive now. Gunther also acknowledged the difficulties of being a doctor: "they seldom, if ever, tell you everything.... [because] there is much, even within the confines of a splinter-thin specialty, that they themselves do not know."

On April 7 I was back in the MRI machine for the first time since the surgery. We had every reason to believe that it would show no new growth, as I had no symptoms, and the first course of chemo had been administered. The psalm appointed for that day was Psalm 31, and verse 24 read, "Be strong, and let your heart take courage, all you who wait for the Lord." I took deep breaths as I sat in Dr. Uhlmann's waiting room following the MRI, again trying not to look around me at other patients who were suffering in much more visible ways.

"The MRI looks good," Dr. Uhlmann said the moment he entered the room, bypassing any other greeting. He always understood that I didn't want to wait any longer than necessary for this news, regardless of other things we would discuss. My first question to him this time was about my prognosis.

"My PCP said that my ten-year survival rate looks good. I had not been thinking about this as terminal."

"I don't think about this as terminal either," he replied. "Anything can happen but you are not average. You are young, you are receiving good treatment, and I don't believe the data; it comes from when this pill [Temodar] didn't exist. You are going to do much better than the average. I don't find the numbers to be helpful." Score one for Dr. Gould.

Dr. Uhlmann asked about my mood because a small percentage of people become angry while taking Keppra (the anti-seizure medication). Sometimes the spouse reports a personality change or notes that this person was always this way but is worse now.

"Another advantage of being single, I suppose," I said jokingly.

"You can keep your secrets," he said with a conspiratorial smile.

On the advice of a colleague, I asked Dr. Uhlmann if he would give me a letter attempting to release me from jury duty for medical reasons. He stepped out to do this and when he returned, he said, "I don't know if this will work."

"It's worth a try," I said.

"Oh, and you should not read this letter. I have been perhaps more dramatic than is necessary." I took him at his word and passed on reading the letter (which did result in excusing me from jury duty).

We spoke for a moment about my work, and he insisted that I do not have a low-stress job. "Performing is very stressful. You only have one chance and it must be right." I am forever amused by the fact that the man who cures brain tumors for a living thinks that my job as a singer/professor is the more stressful one.

In the months that followed, I went through more cycles of treatment and kept trying to hold my life together. Holy Week felt completely different, as did every other seasonal activity. At Easter Vigil when we read all of the major stories of the faith, the guest preacher said that this is the night to tell all of our favorite stories again ("remember the one about the flood?") and to understand that the Easter story changes all of our daily stories, which she called the movie trailers of our lives that we carry around in our heads like little multiplexes. If things aren't going our way, that's not the whole story. I was incredibly moved by this thought, and I felt sure that this tumor was not yet the end of my story.

In May I presented a master class at the Classical Singer conference in San Antonio and I had a helpful conversation with my friend Troy from our days at The Curtis Institute of Music. He wisely pointed out that regardless of looming illnesses, everyone in their forties feels this way about not wanting to do things that aren't important and evaluates what those things are and what their lives and careers should look like from this point on. He encouraged me to be really specific about my dreams for my future. I told him that I don't want my job to define me or to take up all of my psychic energy. I don't want to sing unless it is a new piece for me or a performance with musicians I truly respect. I recall saying that the Brahms *Requiem* was the last large piece on my wish list, because I've been fortunate enough to sing just about everything else.

I continued to try to find ways to talk to people about what was happening. Some friends listened carefully and compassionately, and others had a surprisingly difficult time hearing anything about it. I was most touched by the friends who asked me questions and seemed to truly care about the answers. I understood that for some people, it was easier to just tell me everything would be fine and move the conversation to another topic. Still, this left me feeling lonely from time to time. I knew that ultimately this was something I would be going through myself for as long as it lasted. I felt lucky to have so many people in my life who were able to talk with me about it.

Dr. Uhlmann continued to be a rock for me. I saw him every month for the chemo prescription and we did a new scan every other month. On one visit I asked him about whether or not I could take something for anxiety. Most medications would interact poorly with the chemo, unfortunately, and Dr. Uhlmann felt that exercise would be a much more effective way to manage my anxiety anyway. I told him I could do more on that front, especially since I wasn't experiencing any weight loss on the chemo drugs.

"We don't want any weight loss—you are perfect as you are," he replied. What woman in her late forties doesn't want to hear her doctor say that?

During each and every visit, he took as much time as I needed for my questions. Often he would preface his answer with "this is not my area but . . ." and then have more knowledge about it than any other doctor. When I said I'd been told to prevent diverticulitis by avoiding nuts, seeds or kernels, he said, "That doesn't sound right. You chew your food, no? A high fiber diet is good." He always reiterated that we have every reason to be positive; this is new for me, it will get easier with time, and everything is going well.

My June MRI showed no new growth and this time Dr. Uhlmann described it as "beautiful." I asked him what constitutes beautiful: the tumor is not growing? The tumor is shrinking? He said that great means no activity. There is some scar tissue around the surgical area, and the limitations of the MRI currently in use mean that it shows a signal whether it is scar tissue or inactive tumor cells. The main factor is the comparison to previous scans. Dr. Uhlmann also decided we could skip one chemo cycle in July while I traveled to Michigan and gave a concert back here in Massachusetts.

I also asked about my short-term memory, which seemed a bit fuzzy. I was still reading new tumor growth into every tiny symptom; it would be many months before I stopped panicking every time I had a headache or dropped something with my right hand. Dr. Uhlmann said my memory issues were probably caused by general fatigue and stress. "You have many things on your mind at the moment."

I had noticed that my scar feels particularly sore when it's about to rain which it still does to this day. "I feel like an old sailor since I can tell whether or not it's going to rain," I told him.

He paused to think about that and then said in all seriousness, "You are not old and you are not a sailor." So much for my ability to make him laugh.

In late June I returned to the Up North Vocal Institute in Boyne City, Michigan where I had been teaching for a number of years. I had a panic attack almost immediately when I stepped into our condo and tried to unpack my things. Everything just felt so different because I was so different. Many times during that month I questioned whether it had been a good decision to return. I still needed blood work every week, and Dr. Uhlmann was less than thrilled about my driving sixteen hours each way to get there. He only agreed to it because I would have a student with me.

During the first week of the program I attempted to do the group hike up the hill at Avalanche Bay. This is a fairly easy walk up a wooden staircase, and normally I'm one of the staff members hanging back with the singers who are overweight and struggling to complete the hike. This time I was the very last person up the hill. The students (especially my own) were staring at me with worry, since there was no obvious reason why I should have had so much trouble.

Of course I was there because I was trying to pretend that nothing had changed, and that I could just continue with my life as planned. I kept waiting to feel normal again, like this was just a passing illness, an inconvenience of prescription medications. But every night when my drug alarm went off, signaling that it was time to take Keppra (and Famotidine to help my stomach process the Keppra), I was reminded of the import of it. I was reminded that while I would eventually be able to stop taking these drugs, I will never be free of this. On some nights, I was having a "normal" evening with friends, perhaps having dinner or drinking some wine or playing dominoes, and I'd forgotten that I have a brain tumor. And then the alarm would sound to remind me to take medication. The "drug alarm," as we started referring to it, wasn't at all like a reminder to take an antibiotic for a sinus infection or to take my vitamins. It was a reminder that I have a brain tumor.

I have written extensively about how singers feel when their voices are compromised. Everything in our lives feels colored by the haze of the illness, and nothing looks normal until we are able to sing again. The brain tumor was having a similar effect on me but in a more extreme, more complicated way. I saw myself as fundamentally transformed, and it was impossible to understand how others saw me now. Did they know how much I had changed, and could they see how much I was still changing?

I knew I would have to learn to adapt to feeling like this, because the tumor was not going away like a sinus infection or a bout with laryngitis. Someday I would be able to "end" treatment (the pill chemotherapy) but for the rest of my life, I will continue to monitor this with MRI's and doctor visits, until I either die of something else or this starts growing again and reaches an untreatable stage. I would learn to stop watching every little change in my behavior or in my body. I would associate small lapses in memory with getting older, not as a sign that my tumor had grown. As Dr. Uhlmann said, this was still new, and I would get used to the new reality. But things would never be the same as they were before January 6, 2014.

There were days in Michigan when I just couldn't recover from the pace. I have always been able to function after putting in long hours, and I was often still able to do this. But then the day would come when my body just said *no*. The workload is no heavier than my regular teaching load at BU; in fact, it was considerably fewer hours. But here I worked with five new students each week. The students came to us from such a wide variety of backgrounds that it was much more complicated to teach them. I exhausted myself in trying to diagnose their vocal issues and fix whatever I could in just a few days, not to mention the considerable effort that went into developing trust so quickly. Some of them got it and some of them didn't, and I have always been too hard on myself about the ones that aren't able to grasp what I am trying to do for them. I take too much of the responsibility for the failure on my own behavior and I have a hard time letting things go.

During that time, I wrote:

> It's a beautiful day outside, I can see that,
>
> and I'm inside feeling tired and sad. I have to
>
> remember that we are doing this treatment to
>
> make sure I'll have many other summers to enjoy
>
> my life. This year is different. There's no point in
>
> refusing to acknowledge that.

I made it through the program and through a late July performance, and in August the chemo began again. I was becoming accustomed to the monthly appointments with Dr. Uhlmann, and I increasingly trusted him to help me remain stable both physically and emotionally. I had ongoing problems with the loud MRI machines because some of the techs told me they could not fit the large headphones into the machines. Dr. Uhlmann said I should refuse to get into the machines without the headphones and I should have them page him if it happened again.

At one of my visits he came out to the waiting room himself to bring me back to his office and later when I asked if he wanted to see me walk (part of the usual neuro tests), he said, "No, I have seen you walk, and I trust that you would tell me if there is an issue."

I struggled to understand my prognosis and asked him what I should say when people ask me about this. I had been telling them I don't have cancer. He agreed that this is not a cancer but it can upgrade itself to one, and unfortunately this is a random process. There are no numbers, and some people live for decades with these tumors. An upgrade is not inevitable, but we know that this medication works, and this is why he insisted on going through all of this treatment.

Dr. Uhlmann always asked me if I had any concerts coming up, and always supported my need for the MRIs to be done safely. When I told him I'd be giving a faculty recital this fall but it was not a big deal, he said, "Not for you!" As with Dr. Stephen, I felt empowered because he expressed an interest in my work and saw me as an accomplished professional rather than just another brain tumor patient. Because he is a faculty member at the Harvard Medical School, he understands the pressures of academia. Once when I mentioned the drama of academic politics at my job and said that he must experience some of that himself, he said, "I pay no attention to that." Wise words indeed.

Doctors like Dr. Uhlmann and Dr. Stephen make difficult situations infinitely more manageable for their patients. They do this in the simplest of ways, with the smallest gestures offered in an emotionally honest way. The doctor and author Atul Gawande laid out some of these ideas in his book *Better: A Surgeon's Notes on Performance*, which is relevant to anyone trying to improve job performance:

Better is possible.

It does not take genius.

It takes diligence.

It takes moral clarity.

It takes ingenuity, and above all,

It takes a willingness to try.

1. Ask an unscripted question.
2. Don't complain.
3. Count something.
4. Write something.
5. Change.

In September my best friend Kevin took me on the trip of a lifetime: a week in Paris. (When Dr. Uhlmann approved my travel, he said, "It is good to have a friend like that!") My forty-ninth birthday was just two days before we left, and like everything else, it felt different. I had an amazing time with Kevin in Paris and will always be so grateful for his generosity. We flew first class on Virgin Atlantic, which is something I have always wanted to do. I told him I would have been happy just to fly to the Paris airport and back in first class. We stayed in a beautiful apartment near Notre Dame. Kevin was endlessly patient with my tendency to tire quickly. I felt some guilt about missing a week of school so early in the semester but my students understood why I needed to go, and I made up every lesson. When I returned I was eager to share my new knowledge about singing in French.

I brought back a small gargoyle statue for Dr. Uhlmann, purchased near the Cathedral. The gargoyle was kneeling with his head in his hands. At first Dr. Uhlmann said I shouldn't waste my money. But then he told me he had seen many gargoyles when he was living in St. Louis but none here in Boston. Then he leaned down to look the gargoyle in the eye. "I like him. He is a serious person and he is thinking." Exactly.

In early October I had a reaction following my seventh cycle of chemo. I had been out at dinner with a friend having Italian food, my favorite. I was standing in the hallway outside my kitchen when all of a sudden I threw up without warning. One minute I was standing in my kitchen and the next moment my stomach was all over the hallway floor. During that night I vomited seven additional times. It was complete misery. I would throw up again while I was attempting to clean up the previous round. Because I live alone, I had no choice but to clean it up right away. It didn't happen again after that night but I knew I would have to report this at my next appointment.

On October 18 as I was waiting for my MRI (they are often backed up), I fell into conversation with a woman about my age and her mother. The woman's husband had been diagnosed with a brain tumor in May after experiencing confusion. He also had Parkinson's disease. After his surgery he developed an infection and they had to open up his head a second time (I know from experience that they really only want to do that once). As soon as they took him off the Keppra, he had a grand mal seizure in his PCP's office. They have two children (ages seventeen and nineteen) and his parents live with them. They drive an hour each way to Beth Israel, where they also see Dr. Uhlmann. She told me they liked him. "He's always late but that's because he takes lots of time." Her husband was still unable to work due to confusion and hallucinations. As she told me that he calls her at work to ask where she is and forgets that their son lives at college now, I saw again how lucky I was. This feeling was always followed by the fear that this could be my future. I ran into them later at Dr. Uhlmann's office, where she told me that their MRI was fine and Dr. Uhlmann thought her husband's continued confusion was due to the medication.

My own MRI that day was scheduled at Farr again instead of the usual large basement machines. They were unable to give me the headphones and I had no recourse because there is only one MRI machine at that location. They put towels into the machine with me but those did nothing to protect my hearing. I left with a painful ringing in my ears.

I felt so defeated at this appointment that I hadn't even brought questions for Dr. Uhlmann. I told him about the vomiting. He described my recent chemo dosage as "negligible" (I said it didn't feel that way) and noted that it is unusual for patients to vomit after the cycle. I explained how sudden and violent the episode was. He sat back in his chair, considering the situation.

"We don't have to do all twelve," he thought aloud. "We can stop now. We have done seven and I am comfortable with just doing MRIs now."

I started weeping with sudden, complete relief. Dr. Uhlmann pushed the box of tissues toward me.

He did all of the neurological exams, which I passed, and then we discussed the loud MRI. He apologized and said he had specifically asked his assistant not to book me at Farr. "I feel I have failed you," he said. "Are you eating?"

"All I do is eat," I joked.

"That's very funny," he said without even the smallest hint of mirth. We made a plan to do the next MRI in December.

I left the Brain Tumor Clinic and sat on the bench out by the elevators, weeping quietly. I was totally overcome by the unexpected gift of not having to do five more cycles of chemotherapy. I was just wiping my eyes and getting up to leave when Dr. Uhlmann came out of the clinic. He asked if I was OK and then we both stepped into the elevator. I asked if he was done for the day and he told me he had some business at the hospital first.

On the sixth floor a woman joined us on the elevator. She moved very slowly and with some embarrassment. Dr. Uhlmann told her to take her time. She got out on the fourth floor, still moving gingerly. The doors closed behind her and Dr. Uhlmann looked at me.

"I'm one of the lucky ones, I know," I said. He smiled and said nothing.

In November a major news story hit: a brain tumor patient named Brittany Maynard had taken her own life at the age of twenty-nine. Newly married, she had debilitating headaches for months before she went to the hospital on New Year's Eve. On January 5 (just one day before my MRI), her MRI confirmed that she had glioblastoma multiforme. They performed a craniotomy but the tumor returned quickly. She and her husband moved to Portland, Oregon because assisted suicide was legal there. She waited until November 1 to end her life so that she could celebrate her husband's birthday on October 26. This date was the last day of my chemo treatment as well as my late father's birthday.

The news of her passing hit me hard. Like so many others, I watched her television interviews in the weeks prior in which she talked about her reasons for wanting to choose to exit on her own terms. Her worsening seizures were the primary reason. I wondered if this was my future while simultaneously feeling an odd survivor's guilt over my comparatively good fortune. I was almost twenty years older than she was during the week we were both diagnosed. Why did she get the really bad kind of tumor when I got the relatively easy one, just days apart? There are no answers to these questions.

As the semester progressed, I tried not to obsess about my upcoming MRI in December. I sang a performance with orchestra, I gave a recital, and I tried to lead the voice department as best I could. Thanksgiving came, and while I was grateful for so many things, this too felt different and less comforting than usual. I knew it was because I had changed in ways that were not yet visible to everyone around me. I received a beautiful handwritten letter from my friend Kay back in Texas, which I reread often because Kay was one of the people who seemed to know me intimately from the first time we met even though we have very different lives. I have always been both happy and apprehensive as the holiday season approaches. This year the anxiety side had a big edge.

On Dec. 15 I had my first MRI following the cessation of treatment back in October. The scan showed no new activity and Dr. Uhlmann was definitely relieved as he said it was "beautiful." I teased him about this word choice and he assured me, in his typically deadpan way, that my MRI *is* beautiful. In October he had asked me to let him know if there were any issues. This time I asked him what symptoms I should watch for and his answer was *none*; the films looked good enough that he didn't expect any symptoms to develop and I should not worry. We would do another MRI in two months but until then, I should "try to forget about this."

Both 2014 and my treatment were officially ending, and now I would begin the long, indefinite period of what they call "watch and wait."

> The people who walked in darkness have seen a great light;
> those who lived in a land of deep darkness—
> on them light has shined.
>
> Isaiah 9:2

—3—

SINGING

In my entire life, I sang the way I wanted to six times. The rest of the time I just did the best I could.

—BEVERLY SILLS

People sing as they are, and the music we make is often the clearest reflection of who we really are inside. No one else has your life experiences and your way of looking at things, I tell my students, so be proud of the unique conglomeration of feelings that makes up your life. And then don't be afraid to allow those feelings and experiences to influence your performances.

After the surgery and during the treatment, people frequently asked me if I was still able to sing. The short answer is yes. I can still do all of the things I could do technically (given the increasing shifts that come with age for us all). Am I the same singer I was before? No, and I never will be again. One of my most cherished recordings is a recital I did in Columbus, Ohio with my dear friend Kevin Jones at the piano in November 2013. It was the last performance I did Before the Brain Tumor. There was a carefree spirit in my singing that night and I trusted my instrument completely. Or maybe it just sounds that way from where I sit now.

I have always been ambivalent about my performing. I love to sing and I love all of the preparations and sensations of putting new pieces into my voice. I especially love seeing what my instrument is capable of and "taking this baby out on the highway every now and then" (as I tell my students). The performance side has been a lifelong struggle but not due to common performance anxiety or stage fright. I have been lucky enough with my teachers to be able to trust my technique to do what is necessary in most situations. The real reason is that I am an introvert, and I tend to be quiet and shy unless I feel comfortable with the company I'm in. I don't mind the occasional spotlight but I don't need it as some do. I think of it as something I must endure when I sing a performance: all of those people looking at me and expecting something interesting from me.

I have worked through those feelings by writing two books about how ego issues affect singers, and more specifically, how those issues have impacted my own life in music. Throughout my life I have kept a journal into which I pour my feelings about those issues. I find it enormously helpful to put some of those thoughts into writing for people I don't know. It also helped me to understand that I do my best performing when I don't try to perform, when I'm as honest with my texts as I can bear to be. When I perform a recital, I hope that the audience members leave feeling as though they know me.

The brain tumor amplified all of these emotions. After the surgery, I felt physically vulnerable, not just emotionally vulnerable as I've always been. My body was different, and at first I was apprehensive about how it would perform. When done properly, singing is a fine-tuned physical coordination. Good singers use their whole bodies and don't just sing from the neck up. I was no longer sure how my body would react, or whether the combination of physical and emotional shakiness would prove to be too much. Would I be able to do the technical things I could do before this happened? Could I find the emotional strength to keep going with it after using so many personal resources just to process the diagnosis and surgery? These were the big questions.

I have been singing from the time I was a small child, and my voice is permanently woven into my identity. There was no question in my mind that I would continue through this medical situation. I desperately wanted to believe that nothing had changed in my life as a result of this diagnosis. I needed to keep singing, or at least to try, because I needed to prove that I was still myself. And so I never considered canceling my March 2, 2014 performance of *Annelies,* which has been one of my most important works.

Annelies: The Anne Frank Oratorio (by James Whitbourn) is a seventy-minute work for soprano soloist, choir, and either chamber ensemble or full orchestra, depending on the edition used. Melanie Challenger's libretto includes many texts from Anne's diary, provided with special permission by the Anne Frank Foundation. Challenger also incorporates news reports, Biblical verses, German hymns, and various other short texts. The soprano soloist is not intended to be Anne but she shares Anne's words with the choir, especially the soprano section, and there is a sense in which the soloist represents Anne for the audience. I sang the U.S. premiere (which was also the first performance of the chamber version) in 2007 at Westminster Choir College. James Whitbourn and my longtime mentor James Jordan shared conducting duties.

When I prepared the role the first time, I decided to sing it from memory. Anne's words are incredibly powerful and I wanted to present them directly to the audience without any visual barriers. This beautiful work suits my voice, my skill set, and my temperament exactly. There are high floating lines, places that require impeccable intonation, and passages that warrant a more operatic sound. During our rehearsal process, James Whitbourn told me he appreciated the way I aged her vocally, allowing a more mature sound to enter in later in the work. I replied that his writing is what made that happen. The role is cleaner and simpler at the beginning, and the accompaniment underneath the solo lines (as well as the breadth of the lines themselves) necessitates a fuller production later in the work. Most of all, the solo role requires a willingness to be vulnerable. This helped me to tap into my preferred method for handling any performance insecurities: be emotionally honest with my audiences. I believe this is the main reason I have been closely associated with this piece over the years, and it is how I have learned so much about myself in performing in multiple times. I also believe it was no accident that this piece reappeared in my life during my year of diagnosis and treatment. Anne Frank had much to teach me about courage, perseverance, and faith in life's beauty.

When I learned the piece for the premiere, one section of the piece presented a daunting challenge for me: I found it impossible to sing the final movement without dissolving into tears. "Anne's Meditation" contains a melodic soprano line over the choir which is some of the most lyric material in the work. The modulation from G-minor to B-flat major and then back creates a pathos that never becomes excessive. On the very last page of the work, the choir drops out and Anne is left to sing the final phrases over a simple accompaniment:

As long as you can look fearlessly, fearlessly at the sky,
You'll know, you'll know you are pure within.

— Melanie Challenger

My teacher Richard Croft wisely advised me to sing it over and over again and to allow myself to weep as much as I needed to until

I was essentially "cried out." Then I would be able to find the line of emotion I could sustain without breaking as well as without having to resort to full detachment.

Several years after this successful performance, a soprano with more elite professional connections arranged for a recording of *Annelies* featuring herself in the soloist role. James W. wrote to me personally to inform me that it was happening, and of course I understood why he had to accept this opportunity. This moving, important work deserved a recording. To say I was disappointed not to be involved in the project would be putting it mildly. The recording was nominated for a Grammy award for Best Choral Performance, and I was truly thrilled for my old friend James Jordan. The Grammy brought widespread attention to the piece in the choral community. Following the publication of the chamber edition, *Annelies* began to receive performances around the country.

In summer 2013 I received an invitation from Jamie Kirsch, conductor of Chorus Pro Musica, to sing the work in Boston in March 2014. Jamie had reached out to James Whitbourn, who told him that I had just moved to Boston and he should try to hire me. I appreciated this vote of confidence more than I can say. This would be my first big performance off-campus in Boston, and it would be a chance to sing "my" piece again. I had no idea that I'd be having brain surgery just six weeks prior to the performance date.

When I received my diagnosis, it never occurred to me to cancel this engagement. Normally I would be deep into vocal preparations in January for a March performance, not recovering from major surgery. The fact that I already knew the piece both vocally and musically, having prepared it so thoroughly the first time, made it possible for me to forge ahead. I brought the score with me to the hospital when I went in for the craniotomy. Looking at Anne's courageous words made my own situation seem far less dark. The piece was a lifeline for my recovery, helping me to be strong when I needed to be and helping me to remember my life outside of the hospital.

As I was preparing the work and attempting to normalize my life, I attended a performance that touched me deeply. On February 7 I went to hear the elegant baritone Gerald Finley sing Schubert's *Winterreise* [Winter's Journey] at Jordan Hall. Performing without a score, he inhabited the music so completely that it felt as though he were composing it on the spot. I attended alone and sat in a balcony seat away from others. As soon as he began to sing the first lines of the first song, "Gute Nacht," I began to weep quietly.

Fremd bin ich eingezogen	A stranger I arrived here,
Fremd zieh' ich wieder aus...	A stranger I go hence....
Ich kann zu meiner Reisen	For my journey I cannot
Nicht wählen mit der Zeit,	choose my own time;
Muss selbst den Weg mir weisen	I must pick the way myself
In dieser Dunkelheit.	Through this darkness.

The longing and sorrow in his voice reached into my soul and comforted me. The very color of his tone assured me that I was not alone. By the end of the evening I felt inspired and strengthened to return to my work on *Annelies*.

My first rehearsal for *Annelies* with Chorus Pro Musica was scheduled for Monday night, February 26. I was also scheduled to hear auditions for Boston University's Opera Institute all day, and since I was in my first year as chair of the voice department, I didn't feel I could take the day off to rest in advance of the rehearsal. I sang reasonably well but I was exhausted at the end. In one place during the waltz, I kept singing and Jamie stopped me. "That's *tacet* in my score," he said. I wasn't using the published score but rather the score James Whitbourn had sent me back in 2007. I had complained a bit about the length of time that section stayed in the *passaggio*, so I was pleased to see that he had made this change to offer the soprano some relief. The clarinet part he added also made a greatly improved the choir's tuning throughout the work.

When the performance day arrived, I felt anxious for many reasons. Knowing that so many family, friends, colleagues, and students were coming out to support my return to the stage loaded the performance emotionally. I wrote at the top of the first page of my score:

> The Lord is my strength and my shield;
> in him my heart trusts;
> so I am helped, and my heart exults,
> and with my song I give thanks to him.
> Psalm 28:7

This performance would not be about me but about Anne's strength, faith, and courage. It was extremely cold in the church and I found it nearly impossible to release my body adequately to free my head voice. The emotional content of various lines took on new meaning as I tried, unsuccessfully, not to see them through the lens of my own circumstance:

I found a moment to tell you about it, to realize what had happened to me, and what was about to happen.

Chorus: "We must be brave and trust in God."

As long as this exists, the sunshine and this cloudless sky, how can I be sad?

One who has courage will never die in misery.

And yet when I look at the sky,
I feel everything will change for the better.

Whenever you feel lonely or sad, try going to the loft on a beautiful day and looking at the sky.

—Melanie Challenger

By the time I reached the unbearably beautiful final movement, I was trying not to think at all. I was just trying to breathe, make vowel sounds, and keep going until the end. I was proud of myself for getting through it but I was disappointed with my singing. It felt too soon to have people looking at me as well, and wondering whether my hair was adequately hiding my surgical scar.

When I think back on this performance, I realize I should have been kinder to myself about it. People were moved by the piece and no one cared that I wasn't technically perfect, especially after what I had been through. There was no way I could have been at my absolute best on that particular day. And the truth is that technical perfection is far less important than whether or not the artist has managed to move the audience. Anne's words and James's exquisite music helped me to internalize this in ways I had never been able to before the brain tumor diagnosis.

My next public performance took place at the Up North Vocal Institute in Michigan, where I taught for seven years. I was teaching French repertoire alongside the formidable coach Shannon McGinnis, and on July 12, some of the faculty performed selections at the end of the student concert. We opted to perform "Resurrection" from *Chants de terre et de ciel* by Olivier Messiaen. I certainly could have picked something less demanding, but the text felt strong and powerful to me, and it felt easier to spend more sound vocally than to try to control a softer dynamic. I was well into chemo treatments by this point, although Dr. Uhlmann had allowed me to take this cycle off while I was in Michigan.

I decided that night that I would not be a voice teacher, or a brain tumor patient, or even a singer in the traditionally comparative sense. I would just be a voice serving this piece. I left all of the other baggage behind and just went for it. All was well until I sat down backstage afterward, felled by a sudden, incredibly intense headache. It felt like the brain freeze you get when eating ice cream but magnified exponentially. I scared everyone around me for the few minutes it took for the pain to pass.

Back in Boston, Dr. Uhlmann said this was actually a normal consequence following brain surgery. During the surgery certain nerves were severed. The nerve pain I experienced was the result of the nerves trying to adjust themselves. Normal nerves adjust their sensitivity so there is no pain. When you cut the nerves, they try to figure out the correct amplification. Dr. Uhlmann likened this to the way the old television signal would become very loud and indefinite when the signal was lost, because the signal amplified itself in an attempt to reach the antenna. This explanation made a lot of sense to me. (I'm quite sure that Dr. Uhlmann is an excellent teacher at the Harvard Medical School.) As with the functional MRI earlier,

I would have found all of this truly fascinating if it were happening to someone other than me. Fortunately I never had another similar nerve pain headache.

At the end of July, just a few weeks later, I sang another performance of *Annelies* for the Massachusetts ACDA Convention at Smith College in Northampton. This performance was a joint effort by Chorus Pro Musica, conducted by Jamie Kirsch, and Coro Allegro, conducted by David Hodgkins. I prayed for the strength to negotiate the role again but my fears were unfounded, as I gave my best performance of it up until that point. In March the emotional content was daunting for me as the text took on unsettling meaning. Now I found the emotions empowering. The meaning of Anne's words was no longer something to be avoided but rather I had to give myself to completely. People later said that I inhabited the role and made it my own. I made a few small rhythmic errors but threw myself all in as I had never done before in any performance.

Anne inspired me throughout every word that day. I felt strong when the choir said, "We must be brave and trust in God" because I had seen the power of that trust in my own life. I let myself be Anne, not sad (as James Whitbourn always insisted), and I let myself feel her optimism and humor. The German chorale toward the end, "Ich danke Dir für alles gut, recht und schön [I thank You [God] for all that is good, right, and beautiful]," used to undo me but this time I gained strength from it. There is still so much good in my life, I thought. Waiting in my seat, I prayed for the fortitude to sing the last meditation without falling apart.

When I stood up to begin it, I felt an entirely different mood overtake me. All at once I was able to feel how grounded she was ("I see the world") and I knew what I needed to do. I had to open up my stance and give everything that was in me. Instead of trying to get through it without crying, I focused my gaze on one spot in the back of the hall and opened up the full power of my instrument. I had control I have never had on stage before as well as new generosity of breath and sound. I felt some small participation in Anne's maturity because of what I endured that year, and I felt grounded and sure.

Many years earlier I prayed for God to be with me during a performance of the Bach aria "Öffne dich" (from Cantata BWV 61) with the Dallas Bach Society. I had a devastating sinus infection and was unable to speak but there was no one to take my place so I had to try. The performance went surprisingly well, in part because my technique was on high alert; I had to do everything correctly to have any hope of phonating. Afterward, I understood that God had *always* been with me when I sang. Why hadn't I realized that before?

After the Mass ACDA performance, I knew that *Annelies* was the most appropriate piece to help me find my new path in the world post-brain tumor diagnosis. No text could provide a more profound perspective on life's sufferings and joys than the diary of Anne Frank. Despite my emotional and physical challenges that year, I was able to thrive, and I learned much about my faith and my strength from her. I wrote at the time: "Does God hear these prayers and bring me strength, or do the prayers act as a placebo, giving me strength because I believe they will? Does it matter?" Now that I have more perspective, I believe that God does hear these prayers, and my belief in this truth is what makes the difference.

I went on to sing a number of other *Annelies* performances over the next several years. Anne truly led me through the transition to the new normal in my life. In spring 2015, I sang the work with three different conductors: Rodney Wynkoop (Choral Society of Durham), Robert Eaton (Assabet Valley Mastersingers, in the full orchestra version), and Robert Duff (Handel Society of Dartmouth). I gained a great deal of personal and musical confidence through each of these performances. I was usually the only person in the room who had ever done this piece before, something that just doesn't happen in the field of classical music, so I felt like an expert. I also count the composer as a friend, and I compared notes with him after each performance.

In spring 2016 I sang the work with a high school choir for the first time, Jason Iannuzzi's exceptional Lexington High School Combined Choirs. I was skeptical about whether high school students could negotiate these choral parts, musically or emotionally. Prior to the rehearsals, we had a session in which they asked me insightful questions about how it had been to prepare this role. All of the performances I did were special: Rodney Wynkoop's was a tight, musically superior rendition; Robert Eaton's was the only time I sang it in the full orchestra version; and Robert Duff's was given for a combined audience of high school students from around the region. The Lexington performance surprised me, not just because the choir did such an effective job with the part. There was something extremely poignant about the places in which Anne's text alternates between the soloist and the soprano section. Hearing Anne's words sung by young girls her own age added a new dimension emotionally.

During the *Annelies* performances in the winter and summer of 2014, I was not actively taking chemotherapy pills. In the fall of that same year, however, two other performances I sang fell during the active five-day cycle of taking the pills, not just during the twenty-three days afterward. Both times I carried on as though nothing was different, not due to any superhuman strength but rather due to my steadfast denial of my situation. I have always been hard on myself and this was no exception. I would not allow myself any slack, even for chemotherapy treatments for a brain tumor.

In September I performed just one song, "Mondnacht" from Schumann's *Liederkreis,* Op. 39, for a Boston University School of Music Fall Preview night at the BU Castle. The event was arranged as a cocktail party, with faculty, donors, and students in the lobby area of the Castle, which is an old-fashioned mansion. The nearest audience members were just feet away from me, and there were students lined up all along the stairs and the balcony. I felt totally exposed. My mind felt like it was encased in cotton. The words were there but the ticker tape was running too slowly to ward off unease. The song is short but notoriously difficult. I have no idea how successful my performance was that night. All I wanted was to get to the end so that everyone would stop looking at me and I could finally sit down. The fatigue I felt was overwhelming.

The second performance was much easier, in large part because I sang from backstage. I was doing the soprano solo in the last movement of Vaughan Williams' *Symphony No. 3,* "A Pastoral Symphony," which is intended to be sung from offstage. Because I have a certain kind of vocal timbre, I have often been hired to sing from balconies, backstages, and anywhere but onstage in order to create an angelic effect. The conductor of the BUSO, David Hoose, had asked me to sing this particular solo because of the tuning difficulty. The solos at the beginning and end of the last movement are performed a cappella (without accompaniment) and must be perfectly in tune when the orchestra joins in. Since I have perfect pitch, I enjoy this kind of challenge. I also feel that being the Person Who Sings in Tune takes some of the pressure off of me to be the Person Who Sings with Confidence and Personality.

Singing alone from off stage seemed like an apt metaphor for how I felt at the time. The chemo pills made me feel underwater and otherworldly, set apart from the "normal" world around me. I realized later that this was a false construct. Everyone feels that way from time to time because ultimately we are all sailing our own little boats through life. Because of all of these feelings, I felt safe and comfortable performing this solo and coming out on stage at the end just to take a quick bow.

On November 11, 2014 I gave a previously scheduled faculty recital with my dear friend and musical spirit animal Kevin Jones. Dr. Uhlmann had stopped my chemotherapy just one month before, which was fortuitous because this recital was difficult enough after all my body had endured. I was still pretending I could do everything, and giving myself no room to do any less. If I had the year to do over again, I would be much kinder to myself, and I would have cleared more things from my schedule. But clearly this seemed to be how I needed to handle things at the time. I realize now that this is a very common response to a diagnosis. Public figures such as Beau Biden, John McCain, and Ted Kennedy all kept working on their full schedules as long as possible in order to maintain the sense of purpose that had always defined their lives.

Although Kevin and I repeated two sets from our Columbus recital the previous fall, the Schumann and the Barber, we certainly didn't take the easy way out with the program:

Schumann	*Liederkreis,* Op. 39 (12 songs)
Bouchot	*Galgenlieder* [Gallows Songs] (5 songs)
Barber	*Mélodies passagères* (5 songs)
Messiaen	Selected songs (2)

I remember feeling like this recital was happening to someone else. I was on stage, trying to remain standing and to keep my breath under me, but I was also somewhere outside of the event looking in with curiosity. At some point during the Schumann I asked myself why I had thought I could open with twelve songs all in the middle voice, even though I had done exactly that the last time I sang this cycle. The other sets all felt more comfortable although I was aware of feeling less easy in the Barber and Messiaen than in previous performances of those songs. The Bouchot set was brand new and quite challenging. Listening to the recording of this performance is frustrating to me because I hear a labor and heaviness in my voice that isn't usually there. In subsequent performances of the Bouchot, I have struggled with muscle memory from this first rendition as well. Still I was proud of myself for putting myself on the stage at all and for delivering the program without any major gaffes. I looked forward to returning to complete vocal health, which I hoped would soon follow.

About a year later, I performed a song that resonated deeply with me and my health struggles. "Last Night When I Returned" by the rising musical theater composers Tim Rosser and Charlie Sohne is sung by a woman who is returning to her husband's home as a ghost following her death, and she narrates her feelings as she wanders through his house and discovers that he has remarried and had a child. The stand-alone song was written for the musical theater soprano Rebecca Luker, and it is a rare case of a song set high enough in range for an ingenue soprano voice (which I have) but carries a text suitable for a woman over the age of thirty. As I practiced the song, I knew it was going to be difficult to perform but I also knew that I needed to do it. In a joint recital with two of my BU colleagues, I introduced the song using Rosser and Sohne's own words, calling it a little ghost story. Many of the audience members were familiar with my history, and there were some tears shed that night.

In the years since my treatment, my feelings about my singing have shifted in a new direction. The act of doing it seems less necessary to me now. The physical energy required to do it properly becomes harder to reserve given everything else I have on my professional plate. The mental focus required to perform well is even harder to come by. As one colleague of mine puts it, it is impossible to perform at peak levels when you are doing it part-time. I have increasing administrative duties at school, which makes it less acceptable to take time away from school to perform off-campus. And as a woman in my fifties, I am considerably less marketable as a soloist than I was in earlier years.

This would have been the case with or without the brain tumor. Whether we still sing well or not, we are affected by our society's obsession with youth and flashy new things. It is a little less true for men, to be sure; women "of a certain age" in all of the arts professions commiserate about how hard it is to find work. For example, one staple of my early repertoire, Handel's *Messiah*, fell off my calendar the moment I turned forty, because the soprano soloist must be young and pretty.

In fall 2015 the Americke Jaro Festival [American Spring Festival], based in Prague, hired a new director after longtime director Irina Rybackova retired. Despite my eleven seasons with the festival and the demand for my services at a number of the venues, the new director sent me a brief email letting me know she would be hiring "new younger artists" for her inaugural season. And could I please help her to identify some of these young artists from the United States?

I responded tersely. I hoped the festival appreciated the work I had done to help build it under its current and previous monikers, and while I wished them well, I would be unable to help going forward. I then received a direct appeal from Irina, apologizing for the new director's insensitivity and asking me to supply her with one name out of regard for our own long working relationship. Of course I did, and my student Kelley Hollis, soprano extraordinaire, has done several seasons with the festival at this writing. As I have told Kelley, I hate that I'm not doing it anymore but since it can't be me, I'm happy that she is the one who has the opportunity now.

The end of my association with AJF did not signal the end of my career as a solo performer, of course. I have continued to sing whenever it makes sense to accept the offer. Following my treatment year I added a number of new soprano solos to my curriculum vitae, including *Les Noces* (Stravinsky), *Alexander's Feast* (Handel), *In Childhood's Thicket* (a premiere piece for soprano, baritone, chorus and electronics by Andy Vores), "Infelice" Op. 94 (Mendelssohn) and my bucket list piece, *Ein deutsches Requiem* (Brahms). I have also revisited old favorites such as Haydn's *"Lord Nelson" Mass*, Poulenc's *Gloria,* and Mozart's *Great Mass in C Minor.* I am particularly glad to have a satisfactory recording of the "Et incarnatus est" with orchestra.

I have done much thinking about my singing and what I want from it. One decision I have made is to take on some professional choral work as a regular substitute with the Advent Choir (the all-professional choir at my beloved parish). For me this is highly enjoyable as long as the group and the conductor are on a high level. It is a way for me to continue using my voice and performing in a less personally stressful manner. During my undergraduate years I was fortunate enough to sing under Dr. William A. Payn, who inspired a lifelong love of choral singing (and gave me the tools to do it professionally without compromising my solo technique in any way). I went on to sing with the Philadelphia Singers and then the Dallas Bach Society, with whom I did both solo and choral work for many more years. There is an outdated stigma for professional singers who do choral work but that seems to be changing as more intelligent, stylistically sophisticated young singers are able to make a living that incorporates both solo and choral opportunities. Why shouldn't singers enjoy the benefits of ensemble work just as readily as orchestral players?

As for solo work, at this point I have performed all of the major works on my bucket list (with enormous thanks to Dr. Payn for making the Brahms happen). There are a number of pieces I never need to sing again, as I have said all I have to say about them. While I look forward to more years of great music as a soloist, it is liberating not to *need* any of that work. In my younger years I fretted about how I would feel when things began to slow down. Because of the brain tumor, I have a perspective on life that makes it easier for me now. I see myself and I feel my identity as something more than a singer. I understand that the act of singing is no longer the most important thing I want to do with my remaining time. I have also sought to create my own performance opportunities rather than wait for invitations.

In fall 2017 I gave a recital with my esteemed colleague Javier Arrebola that attempted to honor this new perspective. We called the program "On Aging and the Passing of Time," and chose the following pieces:

Schubert	*Abendröte Lieder* [Sunset Songs], selections
Ullmann	from *Six Sonnets of Louise Labé*
Cipullo	*Of a Certain Age*

Selected songs:
"We Must All Be Very Kind to Auntie Jessie" (Noel Coward)
"Memory" from *Cats* (Andrew Lloyd Webber)
"Forever Young" (Bob Dylan)

This program stirred many feelings in me as a singer and as a woman. There were lines in so many of the songs that brought me to tears as I practiced, and it became a catharsis on a large scale. At the time it felt like I was giving myself permission to stop giving full recitals if I so choose, and to take that pressure away. I also felt all of the feelings of having lived through a life-threatening illness, and the gratitude of still being here to sing about it.

The Cipullo set was particularly satisfying in this regard, and I have kept it in my recital repertoire. All but one of the six poems comes from the work of Lisel Mueller, and all of the texts deal with issues relevant to a woman of a certain age. Perhaps most importantly, Cipullo sets these poems with a keen understanding of a higher, lighter soprano voice. So much of the repertoire appropriate for my voice is based on texts that are really only suitable for a much younger woman, centered on questions such as, "Will I ever meet a boy?" These poems have themes including memories of one's youth, the changing of a woman's body over time, life and death in a nursing home, and a memory of the singer's late mother. Singing this last poem with my own mother (who is very much alive) in the audience was not an easy task. The Cipullo set is a wonderful example of the interesting and relevant repertoire I hope to present in my remaining years as a recital soloist.

Several years ago one of my students asked me if I had any regrets about my performing life. I have just one: I wish my young self could have appreciated my gifts more fully. During my time as a master's student at Curtis, I worked on the seminal coloratura role of Zerbinetta in *Ariadne auf Naxos* (by Richard Strauss). I thought at the time that there were literally hundreds of other sopranos my age who could sing this, and they were all prettier and better actresses than I was. Now that I've been teaching for over twenty years, and I have only had one student to whom I would even consider giving that aria, I know that it was a special gift. It wouldn't have changed anything for me to know that; I was not meant to sing all over the world and would have hated that life. But I would have been kinder to myself and possibly enjoyed it more along the way.

I had an interesting revelation when I attended a performance at the Metropolitan Opera with my best friend Kevin Murray. He joked about when we were young singers dreaming of singing there. I told him that I had always been terrified when I went there as a young singer, because the expectation at Curtis was focused on singing at that particular house. I was deathly afraid that someone would *make* me sing there one day, and I knew I was not nearly extroverted enough for that.

After many years away from The Curtis Institute, I attended a voice/opera reunion there. Since Curtis only graduates about five singers a year, and just a handful of us attended, we were a small group. I was struck immediately by the camaraderie we found in our shared experience. Even though most of the other singers progressed further in their careers before leaving full-time performance (with one exception, Vinson Cole), we all felt the strange dichotomy of life at a high echelon music school: the expectation that we would go on to sing at all of the world's major houses counterbalanced with the suggestion that we might never be good enough to do it. The weekend was healing in every way. It affirmed my career choice, as I quickly saw that temperamentally the others were far better suited to performance careers than I was, and I was grateful to have figured that out fairly early in my life. I also felt a real sense of pride, especially as we were given a private tour of the Anna Moffo (Curtis '54) archives. No matter what I went on to do with my life, no one will ever be able to take my Curtis degree away from me. I will always know in my heart that I was good enough to be accepted into this enormously competitive, tuition-free program.

I hope to continue to sing in as many ways as possible for as long as I can. I have much more to say now and I am far less interested in what other people think about my performances. I have nothing left to prove to anyone, including myself. I can sing now for the sheer love of it and for the communication of beautiful words. I also know that it means something to my students to hear their teacher in performance, and to see me putting myself in the same vulnerable position I expect of them. Every time I open my mouth to sing, I learn something about how to do it, and about how it affects me personally and emotionally. At the end of the day, this knowledge benefits both me and my students in more ways than I know.

STUDENTS

One paints and one draws to learn to see people, to see oneself.

—PABLO PICASSO

The decision to tell my students about my brain tumor diagnosis was an easy one for me. As the author of two books on how personality impacts singing, I knew I couldn't hide my condition or my feelings about it from them and still be the openly empathetic teacher I strive to be. As the Broadway singer Idina Menzel told *The New York Times* (February 23, 2014),

> You can't be the vulnerable, transparent, raw person
> required to be an artist, and then cover that stuff up and
> meet the world with some kind of armor on. It just
> doesn't go.

I can't ask my students to be open, courageous, and vulnerable unless I am willing to be those things myself. This might not have been everyone's choice but it was mine, and it was the right one for me.

During my first studio class following my surgery, with all fourteen of my students gathered, I told them the basics, being careful to preface all of it with the reassurance that all was well. I explained why I'd gone to the hospital and what they found there. The doctors were optimistic that everything would be fine but I would definitely start some sort of treatment later that spring, and I was counting on their patience with me. I promised they would receive every one of their lessons for the semester, including the ones I had already missed. I canceled two concerts of my own, participation in a program at Curtis and a recital I had been planning to give at BU. Later I made it clear that I would not attend as many performances at BU as I normally did. It just wouldn't be possible to do everything, and I was choosing to do their lessons first.

My students handled the news like the incredible young adults they are. Some of them cried a little and others had questions, mostly about what this had been like for me. I took off my cap and let them see the healed scar. Some of them hugged me. Many of them commented later on how much it meant to them to know that they were my priority even while dealing with something like this.

Throughout this experience, I have received much advice, both solicited and unsolicited, about whether or not I should share the news with my students. Not everyone would choose to inform their students about something this personal, fearing that it would weaken them in the eyes of the students or frighten them unnecessarily. I didn't mention a word of it prior to the surgery; I told our department assistant to just tell them I was having some tests done if anyone asked. But once I returned to school, I had to offer some explanation for missing the first two weeks of the semester as well as for wearing a hat indoors. And once treatment started, I would mostly likely be unable to keep this situation completely hidden.

During the chemotherapy semester, my students were a daily blessing for me, and I tried as hard as I could not to scare them or to make them feel responsible for taking care of me. Their youth and enthusiasm for singing inspired me and gave me strength. Most of all, I was grateful for the chance to focus on something other than my health. I threw myself into the lessons and only missed a few days at school. I posted a sign-up sheet for make-up lessons and fulfilled every one of them.

The students reacted to my treatment in a variety of ways. Most of them approached their time with me gently and with extreme kindness, which I appreciated on a very deep level. There were a few who never made any reference to it at all, and it was as though I had never told them. At the time I was somewhat hurt by that but now I understand that this was the way they needed to compartmentalize things, and I also see that it must have been uncomfortable for them.

Only one student reacted in an openly negative way. Toward the end of the semester, this student inquired about postponing their recital to the fall semester because they didn't feel adequately prepared. Not coincidentally, this same student had not signed up to make up the few lessons I had missed. I pointed that out and also informed the student that their grade for the semester would reflect this lapse.

"Does the fact that you weren't there for me this semester play into this at all?" the student asked defensively.

I must admit, not proudly, that upon hearing this I became as angry as I have ever been with a student.

"How dare you," I lashed out. "I missed ten days of school for a brain tumor, not a sinus infection, and I posted make-up times for every single lesson. The fact that you didn't sign up or make other arrangements with me is entirely on you."

The exchange ended with us both wiping away hurtful tears. It was hardly my finest moment as a teacher. I have thought about that day many times over the intervening years. While I wish I had not become so angry, I can now forgive both myself and the student for experiencing a moment of intense humanity.

After it became clear that I would have to undergo treatment, I decided to reach out to some former students from my years at the University of North Texas. I didn't want any of them to hear about the tumor by accident and leap to dire conclusions. In 2014 social media already held formidable power. I had not posted anything on FaceBook about this but I knew that word might get out fairly quickly. I sent private messages to about ten or twelve students with whom I had been particularly close, asking them to call me when they had a moment so that I could share some news with them.

I heard from all of them within a week or so. Those phone calls were difficult but also life-affirming. I called out of concern for them but the support they gave me was overwhelming. It was empowering to be back in touch with these exceptional people, and to be offered a glimpse of the adults they had become. One asked me how comprehensive my health insurance coverage was and asked if he should put together a benefit concert for my medical expenses. (I politely declined; my university insurance is excellent.) Another seemed to take the news with equanimity but the following evening I received a call from his mother, who wanted to confirm that my prognosis was truly as positive as I had led her son to think. (As a college professor I don't interact with parents all that often but there are some who attend so many of their child's performances that I come to know them in a circumstantial way.) Another of these students took great care to arrange Skype calls with me often during the next two years even though he was teaching in China at the time. Talking with these students helped me to see the legacy I already had, no matter what was to come next.

In the years since my initial diagnosis, I have made it my practice to tell new students individually about it at a moment that feels organic. I do this early on for the same reason I called my former students: I don't want them to hear about "Dr. E.'s brain tumor" through a casual mention at a party. With each uneventful year I am more easily able to present it in a non-threatening way. I let them know that I occasionally need to miss school for an MRI because the scheduling is not usually my choice entirely. Most students are surprised at first but then glad to hear that everything is fine. It undoubtedly leads them to see me in a slightly different light but I think that is normal. My students are old enough to handle this kind of information. They are all over the age of eighteen, and most of them are twenty-two years old or older.

In one of these conversations, the subject of my brain tumor arose because this student had just accepted a choral position at my church and he was glad to learn that I was a Christian. Learning this about me made him feel that God had placed him in the right university program after all (since BU had not been his first choice). As we spoke about my diagnosis, I told him that I had faith that I would be all right, at least for now. He responded, "You will be," with such a deep sense of calm that I felt it must be true. Both the discussion about our shared faith and the fact of the diagnosis cemented our mentor/student relationship in its own unique way.

As an educator I have wrestled with the question of how to treat my students equitably while recognizing that it is virtually impossible to treat each one in exactly the same way. The one-to-one nature of studio teaching means that the dynamic in the room is specific to each student by definition. They are distinct individuals of different ages, backgrounds, personal styles, life experiences, and, yes, skills and talents. It is not possible to interact in exactly the same manner with every single student; at least, it's not possible within my intentionally empathetic teaching style. I try to know my students well enough to know what they can handle on any given day, and to help them reach the next musical step in their lives, whatever that might be. Some will go on to graduate school or performance careers, some will become administrators or teachers, and some will choose a different life altogether. I hope that each and every one of them knows how sincerely I care about them as people and how hard I work to help them determine what they want from music.

I have always seen teaching voice as a holistic activity. I am not the kind of teacher who focuses exclusively on anatomical information and keeps things on a practical, impersonal level at all times. There's nothing wrong with that approach, and there will always be students who prefer more emotional distance. It's just not the way I am built, for the same reason that I have never been able to sing in a presentational, intentionally performative way. In the performance world, there have long been two types of singers, the emotional and the presentational, and I do not think it's possible to change one's personal tendency. Whenever I distance myself from the text and the musical meaning and try to "perform," I make mistakes. In the teaching studio I have the same difficulty. I believe it is possible to be both professionally clear and emotionally engaged. This is especially necessary when dealing with singers, who are attempting to communicate with voices that are located, for better or worse, within their very persons.

In thinking about how the brain tumor experience changed me as a teacher, I realized that I could not write about it without some perspective from the other side of the piano. I reached out to some of the students who went through it with me, and I was stunned by their responses. All of them seemed to agree that while they did not notice a big change in the effectiveness of their lessons, sharing in the experience of my diagnosis helped them to mature as adults and to see their own lives in a more complete, well-rounded way. One student said that I helped her to understand that there is more to life—both mine and hers—than singing, and this realization helped her through a medical crisis of her own. I had encouraged her to follow her gut and her heart rather than try to guess what the best "career move" might be. Another said she had never seen me treat two students alike or expect the same things from two people, but I had always respected each student's own journey.

I am confident that the experience has made me more deeply empathetic towards students' personal challenges, particularly those of a medical nature. No situation illustrates this more vividly than the story of my student Mary.

Mary joined my studio as a sophomore in fall 2017. We bonded quickly over our shared geography (we both hail from Long Island, New York) and our love for musical theater repertoire. Our work together was off to a fine start but she had started complaining of fatigue and of feeling pain around her collarbone. On November 1 she was diagnosed with stage II Hodgkin's lymphoma at the tender age of just nineteen. This began a long, difficult year for Mary as she endured eleven rounds of ABVD chemotherapy (the physically intense intravenous kind, not the chemo-lite pills I was given). She lost her hair, suffered from nausea, and fought through jaw pain. Throughout all of it, she continued to come to her lesson every Monday morning at 10:00. Some days she would be able to sing. On other days, she would try bravely (and often insistently) and I would then tell her as gently as I could that I didn't want her to develop muscle memory "workarounds," so we should take things easy that day.

Those Monday mornings were an honor for me but they were also emotionally challenging. I wanted more than anything to do whatever I could to help her, but I was hardly ever sure what form that help should take. I knew that my own experience made me attuned to her needs in a special way but I was also acutely aware of how much more difficult her situation was. I couldn't imagine facing down a potentially life-threatening illness at her age, having had enough trouble myself in my late forties, never mind dealing with the hair loss and other losses of vanity while attending college. There were mornings I had to talk myself into going to school. There were other mornings when I struggled so hard to keep my emotions together during her lesson that I had to ask the next student to give me a moment before starting her lesson. I am forever grateful to that student for her patience as well.

As the weeks passed, I witnessed the awe-inspiring beauty of Mary's spirit as she attempted to keep her life on its normal path. She took the loss of her hair with grace and humor, and she always brought a smile to her lesson because she truly loves to sing. I know that teaching her was an enormous privilege as I had the weekly opportunity to see her life force shining brightly through her hardships. I understood that she wanted things to be as they had been before her diagnosis, because I had the same prayer for myself. I also knew she would experience some dark nights of the soul. But together we kept singing every Monday morning.

In my faculty recital about two weeks after Mary's diagnosis I performed Tom Cipullo's powerful song cycle *Of a certain age,* in which the fifth song is called "Mary." The poem by Lisel Mueller describes the ways in which an old woman (Mary) in a nursing home faces her impending death, stripping herself of the emotions that drive our earthly lives. At the end of the poem she slips into death "the way a swimmer eases into freezing waters," one body part at a time. The very last line of the song calls for the singer to whisper the word "collarbone." The collarbone happens to be where my student Mary's tumor originated.

I spoke with Mary about this prior to the recital and sent her a copy of the poem. I told her I would understand if she wanted to step out of the Concert Hall for this set. I didn't want her to be caught off guard by these highly emotional words, which would undoubtedly resonate with her. Her reaction was characteristic: she would be fine, thanks for letting her know. I wasn't nearly as confident that I would be fine.

The moment of that song in the performance was one I will always recall as though it was just yesterday. As I whispered the word "collarbone," I felt something crack inside me. I was keenly aware of Mary's presence in the room. I was also aware that my mother was in the audience I turned to the final song in the cycle, "The Garden," an exquisitely beautiful recollection of one's mother's permanent place within the ground. Tears gathered in my eyes and I looked down in an attempt to collect myself.

As the seconds ticked on, my feelings only intensified, and I could sense the fear in the room that I would not be able to recover. The silence lasted too long to be normal. Eventually I realized I would just have to forge ahead even though I was still crying. It was one of the most challenging moments of my life as a performer. I was completely unable to separate myself from the empathy I felt for Mary, my mother, and everyone else in the room with knowledge of our situations.

Mary had two colleagues in my studio from her class year, and these three sopranos were the very best of friends. Mary's diagnosis impacted all three of them, and I was cognizant of their need for solace and understanding. I was greatly impressed by the way the three nineteen-year-old sophomores weathered this huge challenge together. There were a number of emotional lessons with the other two young women during that year as they turned to me with feelings they were reluctant to unload on their sick friend.

One of these fierce young women recently shared a memory of that time which I will quote directly in order to preserve her clear voice.

In my very first lesson with Dr. Eustis, she shared some details of her experiences with cancer—a disease whose acquaintance has been made by far too many. Still grieving the very recent and all too sudden loss of my uncle to pancreatic cancer, I appreciated her transparency. Oddly enough, cancer metastasized to another realm of my life later that semester when my close friend and fellow studio member, Mary, was diagnosed with cancer. Her diagnosis at the young age of nineteen shook us all, and, we, as her studio-mates and friends, spent the following spring watching her body and spirit crumble as she endured treatment after treatment. Her tenacity and strength, however, never faltered, and she was declared cancer-free in the summer of 2018.

Mary shared her diagnosis with the studio shortly before our holiday studio party, an annual event to which we are all asked to bring a poem to share with the group. Recognizing how thematic cancer had been in my life recently, I decided to share some rather poetic words that my aunt had shared about her husband (my uncle) when he passed. After everyone had shared their poetry and migrated to the kitchen for dessert, Mary and I lingered in the living room. She thanked me for sharing my aunt's words, and I told her that I had shared them for her. We hugged, sobbing into each other's arms for a few minutes, Mary anticipating the trials of the battle ahead and I recalling the cancerous hardships endured by my loved ones, when Dr. E came up behind us and embraced us both. She reassured us that everything would be alright with the authority of someone who understood exactly what we both were feeling. It is a moment that I think I will remember for the rest of my life and return to for strength in the face of adversity. In that moment, Dr. E showed me that a voice teacher is much more than just that.

In a conversation with Mary for this book, which she wholeheartedly supported, I spoke with her for the first time about how her illness had affected me. I shared my concern that I might not have said or done the right things during her year of illness and treatment. She reassured me that she was grateful for two things. First, I hadn't pitied her or told her that her voice was sounding perfect just to make her feel better. And I hadn't pried; she knew I was there if she needed me but I didn't make her talk about it. I was beyond relieved to hear this. I told her about how I had burst into tears when she left the room following her jury that year, and she was greatly moved. At this writing, Mary is cancer-free and heading to graduate school in New York.

Since the brain tumor diagnosis, I have become both more and less patient with my students. As I said above, I am more empathetic to their personal and medical challenges. I definitely think that students are more inclined to confide in me after hearing about my own situation. Does this make them better singers? It's hard to say. I think it deepens them as artists, though, and allows them to be more vulnerable in life as well as on stage. Renewed patience on my part helps me to be a little less judgmental and unforgiving than I might have been before this happened. My Virgo, detail-oriented side means that I sometimes come across as cold or uncaring, because I am focused on the practical improvements I want my students to make. The tumor has helped me to balance that with my warm, emotionally open side.

On the other hand, I am far less patient with behavior I see as either dispassionate or undisciplined. I experience time differently now, and I don't want my students to wait to become excellent. If they truly desire to pursue a career in the performing arts, they have no time to waste. While I have always tried to steer people away from the career if I think they lack the drive, I am perhaps more direct with them now about what I think they will need to address emotionally before pursuing it. This also means that I have become more discerning about the personalities I accept into my studio, because I know that both of us will do better if our styles match fairly closely.

Sometimes I have made the mistake of thinking that the tumor is not on my students' minds anymore following the initial conversation I had with each one of them. In fall 2019 I told the class that I would be on sabbatical for the spring 2021 semester. I was so worried about disappointing them that I became emotional before I could get the words out. I said I had something difficult to tell them. (Yes, I actually said that without thinking of what it might mean to them.) When I finally articulated the news about the sabbatical, several of them burst into tears. One said, "We thought it was going to be about your health."

Talking to students about our personal issues can be a slippery slope. But there are times when it is absolutely necessary, and their comfort and success in dealing with it depends on how we present things. Singing is a highly personal activity, and it is not possible for either singer or teacher to remain completely objective and emotionless. I might even argue that some may hide even deeper levels of emotion by insisting on maintaining a strict personal boundary. I believe that attitudes around secrecy are shifting rapidly, and I hope that my students feel inspired by my willingness to be honest with them about something that is difficult for me. Our life experiences cannot help but change us in all aspects of our lives. We bring the people we are into our singing, and it follows that we bring the people we are into our teaching as well, whether we realize it or not.

NORMAL

It seems
our own impermanence is concealed from us.
The trees stand firm, the houses we live in
are still there. We alone
flow past it all, an exchange of air.

—RAINER MARIA RILKE, from *Second Duino Elegy*

"This is new for you," Dr. Uhlmann said about five months into my treatment. "It will become normal with time."

With that statement, it fully dawned on me that I would not ever walk away from this and simply return to the life I had before. I would have to adapt to the proverbial new normal, one in which the brain tumor would always be a shadow in the background. Until, of course, or if, it upgrades itself to the forefront again. Finding equilibrium in my new situation became my task during the two years following my treatment.

On January 7, 2015, I threw a party to celebrate the passage of one year from my initial diagnosis. On one of the coldest nights of the year I was joined by many friends, including one who made a special effort to get there (you know who you are; thank you again, my dear friend). I made a playlist for the party in iTunes (because that's what you did before Pandora, Spotify, and other streaming services replaced the mix tape). I titled the list "Epiphany Party" and included some of my favorite songs but also some black humor titles:

"Not Your Year" and "Not Dead Yet" (The Weepies)

"Time to Move on" (Tom Petty)

"Shake It Off" (Taylor Swift)

"Can't Cry Anymore" (Sheryl Crow)

"Brave" (Sara Bareilles)

"Keep Your Head Up" (Andy Grammer)

"It's the End of the World as We Know It" (R.E.M.)

"Hang On, Little Tomato" (Pink Martini)

"Just Fine" (Mary K. Blige)

"Wasn't Expecting That" (Jamie Lawson)

"Things Can Only Get Better" (Howard Jones)

"Closer to Fine" (Indigo Girls)

"Fight Another Day" (Brandon Heath)

"Be OK" (Ingrid Michaelson)

I wrote in my journal that it felt like a birthday. I hoped that I was closing the door on this chapter of my life, evidence of the remaining traces of my denial. The real emotional work of figuring out how to live with this was just beginning. I had to learn how to stop waiting for the other shoe to drop.

Two things happened after that night: (1) suddenly brain tumors were everywhere, and (2) I started reading everything I could find about them. I had no idea there were so many different types, each with its own symptoms, treatment, and prognosis. News reports about celebrity diagnoses seldom specified anything beyond "brain tumor," so I searched deeper into the Internet for details that would help me keep my own diagnosis in perspective. I knew that glioblastoma multiforme is the most lethal variety. In fact, one of my former classmates from high school died just days before my Epiphany party after an amazing four years from his diagnosis.

Ted Kennedy and John McCain both suffered from glioblastoma multiforme tumors. And of course, Brittany Maynard received her glioblastoma multiforme diagnosis within days of my first MRI.

Brittany Maynard's story hit me hard and still invokes deep emotions in me at this writing. A young woman just twenty-nine years old, she had been experiencing terrible headaches, severe enough to cause vomiting, for almost a year. Since this was the first year of her marriage, her doctor ignorantly told her these were "women's headaches" which would fade once she had a baby. On New Year's Eve 2013 she reached a breaking point and was finally given the MRI that revealed a large lesion on her left prefrontal lobe, the same location as mine. Maynard was told it was inoperable and while it presented as a low-grade glial tumor, "historically these evolve into malignant gliomas." Maynard seemed to intuit right away that nothing could be done and she immediately began making plans to move from California to Oregon, where physician-assisted suicide is legal. The night before her craniotomy she made a video asking for death with dignity in case she lost her facilities during the surgery. She was far more rational about her situation than I was. I never considered the possibility that I might not be the same person when I woke up, or that I might not survive the surgery.

Maynard's prognosis was never as hopeful as mine. Her histology report showed that she did not have the combined chromosomal loss of 1p and 19q, so the pill chemotherapy I had was not an option for her. By March her scans showed that her tumor had grown twenty percent larger in just ten weeks. She spent most of her remaining time taking trips and moving to Portland, Oregon to arrange for her end. She began having seizures and the medication to slow these caused her to gain weight. She did several television interviews as well as an interview with *People* magazine to advocate for Death with Dignity laws in more states so that terminally ill people would not be forced to move. On November 1, 2015, after her husband's October 26 birthday but before her own thirtieth birthday (which would have been November 19), she went for a walk in the woods. When she came home, she took a lethal dose of pills surrounded by her family and friends.[1]

In reading Maynard's story, I was struck by how candidly she spoke about the realities of her condition, even when those around her clearly did not want to discuss it. As other cancer patients have noted, it is very difficult when our loved ones are unable to talk about our diseases and push us to bring everything "back to normal" because this is over now. When the poet Nina Riggs' husband told her he couldn't wait for this to get back to normal, she told him:

> I can't handle you saying that. Thinking that way kind of
> invalidates my whole life right now. I have to love these
> days in the same way I love any other. There might not be a
> "normal" from here on out.

Riggs was diagnosed with an aggressive but treatable breast cancer at the age of thirty-seven. Within a year her cancer became terminal, and during that year her mother also died of breast cancer. Her book *The Bright Hour* is a beautiful account of her time with friends and family as she came to accept her own impending death.

Both of these brave women, as well as others whose accounts I have read, shared a willingness to face their diagnoses directly and a sense of frustration when others around them were reluctant to let them articulate their feelings about it. In the days and months following the end of my treatment, I too struggled with finding a way to discuss my feelings without being encouraged to think about it as simply in the past. I didn't think it was being overly negative to want to think through the situation in a more thorough way. I began to read as many memoirs and books about brain tumors as I could find. I was trying to put[1] my situation into some kind of manageable context (not just black and white) and to find some community, although this is not a club anyone wants to join.

One of the first things I learned was how many kinds of brain tumors there actually are. Most people think of brain tumors as serious and immediately fatal, but the truth is that people can survive for years with some of the varieties. The British neurosurgeon Henry Marsh's fascinating book, *Do No Harm: Stories of Life, Death, and Brain Surgery,* contains twenty-five chapters, each bearing the title of a different form of brain tumor. My own tumor, oligodendroglioma, appears very late in the book as Chapter 24. I read Dr. Marsh's case descriptions of each tumor with the excited fear of someone rubbernecking at the scene of a car accident. Dr. Marsh confirmed what I already knew about neurosurgeons—they are incredibly brave, brilliant people—but he also shared the personal, human side of his profession. Patients don't always see this side, and I understand why. When you are facing a brain tumor, you want your doctor to be sure of himself in every way, and you desperately need to see both confidence and superhuman skill. As Dr. Marsh describes these cases, most people find out they have a brain tumor when they experience symptoms such as extreme headaches, blurred vision, balance problems, altered personalities, and seizures.

Dr. Marsh's book also highlights the enormous role luck plays in treating all of these conditions. I was lucky, for example, that I was diagnosed before I experienced any discernible symptoms. Some

---

1 Following Brittany's death, her mother Deborah Ziegler wrote a touching book about her life and decision (Wild and Precious Life).

people live for years after surgery, while others never recover from their surgical procedures. In many cases, it seems impossible for the doctors to predict which course a particular tumor will take. As positive as Dr. Uhlmann always is with me, he also qualifies his positivity by saying, "Anything can happen." Reading about Dr. Marsh's cases underlined that point in a way that was both frightening and reassuring. In all of my reading, I searched for signs I could point to that would give me answers about my future. Sure, that patient died, but their case was different than mine because . . . (fill in the blank). I found very few case studies listing an oligodendroglioma in my other reading so I read Dr. Marsh's chapter closely.

The first sentence of Chapter 24: Oligodendroglioma (subtitle "n. a tumour of the central nervous system") made me catch my breath. Dr. Marsh describes the three operations he has scheduled for the next day, one of which was on "a young doctor with an oligodendroglioma that I had already operated on some years earlier which was now growing back again and which we both knew would ultimately prove fatal."

The patient was an ophthalmic surgeon in his early forties with three young children. After having just one seizure, he learned of his tumor and had surgery, but "the analysis showed it to be of a type that would eventually grow back in a malignant form." (I hung on this sentence as well. How could I know if my tumor was of a similar type?) They had hoped the tumor would take longer than just five years to recur (five years?!?). Dr. Marsh notes how different it is to treat doctors who understand their prognoses better than the average person. Then he writes, "I cannot even begin to imagine what I would think or feel if I knew that a malignant tumour was starting to destroy my brain." Reading this, I was touched by the reality that our doctors are human beings, and that our conditions have an effect on their emotions.

I was comforted by Dr. Marsh's description of his outpatient clinic, which he calls "an odd combination of the trivial and the deadly serious." That is exactly how I experience Dr. Uhlmann's waiting room. We are all there to hear the verdict but we are in different stages of a mysterious, unknowable process. I have often wondered how Dr. Uhlmann faces those conversations two days a week. He has always been quick to tell me that nothing has changed, because he knows that everything else he will say to me is of little consequence. How does he manage on a day when he has bad news to deliver?

During the winter and spring of 2015, some other events challenged my perception of my situation. Anyone living in New England that winter will always remember it as "Snowpocalypse," "Snowmaggedon," or a host of other unprintable names. The first snow of the season didn't fall until January 24 but it was virtually nonstop from then on. We had four blizzards and various other storms for a record-breaking total of 108.6 inches. Sustained temperatures below freezing ensured that the snow never melted between storms. The trains weren't running, cars were buried for six weeks, and snow was eventually dumped into Boston Harbor because there was no other place to put it. Sidewalks were piled high with feet of snow and tiny one-person-wide pathways were shoveled out. I started ordering sundries on Amazon Prime because I couldn't get my car out to go shopping, and taxi drivers refused to come down my street for fear of getting stuck. BU was closed on five separate days.

With everyone snowed in for so long, I'm sure I was not the only person in an especially reflective mood. Then in April my beloved little black cat Annie died of a brain tumor (of all things). I had to put her down on Maundy Thursday. The next day one of my Catholic students joked that I would only have to wait two days to see Annie again on Easter Sunday. I actually laughed; that's how dear this particular student was to me.

At the end of May the world learned that Joe Biden's son Beau had died at the age of forty-six from a brain tumor, which had been diagnosed two years earlier. Beau Biden was misdiagnosed with a mild stroke in May 2010 after having a headache, numbness, and paralysis. The doctors at the renowned University of Texas MD Anderson Cancer Center in Houston eventually diagnosed his glioblastoma multiforme tumor in August 2013. He had surgery and treatment but was admitted to Walter Reed just ten days before his death. Between Beau Biden's outstanding record of service to our country and his father Joe's eloquent tributes, the coverage of Beau's death was widespread.

Less than one month later, news broke that the Russian operatic baritone Dmitri Hvorostovsky had been diagnosed with a brain tumor and would cancel all of his summer engagements. Few details were available, even on the classical singer underground network. Hvorostovsky has long been one of my very favorite singers, a consummate artist with a voice that wraps itself around you like a giant fur coat. Early in my teaching career, I took a small group of my graduate students to hear his Cliburn Series recital at Bass Performance Hall in Fort Worth. We joked that we were going to throw our bras onto the stage to honor him as the rock star he was to us.

In November 2016 Hvorostovsky gave an extensive interview to TASS, the Russian News Agency, about his condition. He spoke of taking time on his own to process his diagnosis despite being a much-loved celebrity:

It's important to understand the psychological condition of a person who has just learned about one's illness, possibly a lethal one. At such moments you don't feel like socializing with anyone.

We gladly share joy and happiness with the world around us, but when we are in trouble, it's better to stay alone. Getting accustomed to the new realities is far easier when there is no one around. You must get over it on your own. Nobody will help. Nobody will ever manage, however strong the wish to help may be.

His doctors assured him that he would be able to remain on stage and lead an active life: "You won't die." Hvorostovsky went through chemo and radiation and eventually returned to the stage. But he continued to experience balance issues, and in December 2016 he withdrew from the operatic stage completely. In May 2017 he made a surprise appearance at the Metropolitan Opera Gala celebrating fifty years at Lincoln Center, singing "Cortigiani, vil razza dannata" from Verdi's *Rigoletto*. Bent over in the role of the hunchback jester, he gave a brave, memorable performance and received tears and ovations. He continued to give recitals but in November 2017 he passed away in London at the age of fifty-five.

As a way to bear all of this news, I began to read and write even more intensively, and to turn to my faith for strength. Psalm 90:12, 14–15 reads:

> So teach us to count our days
> that we may get a heart of wisdom.

> Satisfy us in the morning with your steadfast love,
>
> that we may rejoice and be glad all our days.
>
> Make us glad for as many days as you have afflicted us.

I grappled with what that might mean. How could I use the counting of my days to teach my own heart to live with gratitude instead of fear? Reading the Daily Office, the discipline of it, helped me to internalize the idea that all of life's dramas are fleeting but God is eternal. Even though I believed this to be true, I struggled to find signs in my daily life that would support the long view. How could I, as a college professor, find authentic strength in something that so often seems contradictory to the reality of the world?

During Holy Week I was on my way to the Tenebrae service at The Church of the Advent when I had the chance to do something special for someone. The experience felt like hard evidence for the existence of the spiritual world. I wrote about it at the time and have included that writing here in its original form.

It happened during Holy Week, on Wednesday night just after 6:30 in the Public Garden. I was headed to The Church of the Advent in Beacon Hill for the Tenebrae service, which was scheduled to begin at 7 pm. I was planning to take the 6:22 Green Line-C train from St. Mary's Street to Arlington but as I walked up to the station, the 6:15 arrived. I figured I'd just take a leisurely walk through the Public Garden for once (foregoing my typical sprint to make it to our pew before the processional starts).

I was just inside the gate of the Garden (Boylston and Arlington corner) when a teenager, maybe 15 years old, 16 at the most, approached me. He was wearing a hooded gray sweatshirt, jeans, and sneakers, but no coat. It had been 63 degrees earlier in the day but as night was falling, so was the temperature. He had red hair. His eyes were red as well. At first I wondered if he was homeless or on drugs (red eyes?) but I quickly realized that he had been crying.

He asked if he could use my phone, saying it was an emergency. "You can hold your phone while I call." Hesitantly, I reached inside my bag and said, "OK. What is it you need?"

"I need to call my uncle. I was getting on the train with my friend but it was crowded and he made it on but the doors closed on me."

His hands shook as he pulled a tiny slip of paper out of his pocket. The uncle's number was written down just before his phone battery died. He held all of his pocket cash over my phone, and said, "Thank you so much," as he tried to dial with cold fingers.

"Of course. I know how hard it is when you can't find a way to solve your problem."

He looked up at me. "*So* many people said no. I've been out here asking for like twenty minutes at least."

He stepped slightly away to make the call and I circled around him a bit nervously. What if he decided to take off with my phone? I need a new phone anyway, I thought randomly. But he looked so scared, and I sensed that he was really in trouble. No one answered the phone so he gave it back to me and said thanks anyway as he started walking out of the park towards the Taj Hotel. I wished him luck and headed towards church.

Something stopped me, though, and I had a strong feeling that this was not the end of the story. I thought, What if the uncle didn't answer because he didn't recognize the number? If the kid tries a few more times, maybe the uncle will figure out that it's not a robo-call. I began walking faster to catch up with the kid out on Arlington Street.

I yelled out, "Hey!" and he heard me the second time. I motioned him over and explained what I was thinking.

He gladly took the phone but there was still no answer. I couldn't just leave him there so I asked him where he needed to go.

"Do you know if there are any motels around here?" he asked.

"Um, there are a lot of hotels here. Which one are you looking for?"

"That's the problem: I don't know the name of our hotel. Did I tell you we were trying to go to Quincy Market? I got in a cab and he just dropped me here."

I asked if he would recognize a picture of the hotel.

"Yes, if I could see where you go when you come out of the elevator. It's a really tall hotel [I smiled] and there's a place where you drive in to park your car and then you take an elevator to the lobby. I'd definitely recognize the lobby. It had really ugly couches."

I laughed and said, "That narrows it down. A hotel with ugly couches." He laughed a little bit too. I started Googling hotels and showing him pictures—the Westin Copley, the Residence Marriott Fenway. Then he said it was near a fire station so I showed him the Sheraton Hynes. That wasn't it either.

"There is definitely a pool. I wish I could show you the picture I took from our room but my phone is dead." Poor kid—if he could show me the picture, he wouldn't be talking to me in the first place.

My phone kept taking forever to load each image so I apologized for how slow it was. He said, "No problem. I'm just so glad you stopped."

"I was heading to church but I had a feeling. I travel a lot and I know how it feels to be lost in a foreign city. You didn't look scary to me. You just looked lost and cold."

"I'm *so* cold," he said sadly.

I was trying to think of what to do. Maybe I could put him in an Uber to one of these hotels where at least he'd be inside and able to use a phone? I told him to try his uncle again. This time the uncle picked up.

"Mark?" the kid said anxiously. I heard him ask what hotel it was (Hilton Back Bay) and Mark must have asked where he was because he said, "I'm here with a lady who's helping me." I motioned for the phone. "She wants to talk to you."

"Hi, I'm Lynn," I said. "I'm here with your friend trying to get him back to you. I'm going to put him in an Uber to the Hilton. Does that sound OK?"

Uncle Mark said, "That would be great. He should have money he can give you."

"Don't worry about it, I've got it."

"That's very kind of you, thank you." Uncle Mark's voice broke a little.

While I was ordering the Uber on my phone, I told the kid I was sorry I didn't know all of the hotels. I live here so I don't stay in them often.

He said, "Wow, do you even *have* a car?"

"Yes, but I don't drive it very often, and I didn't drive tonight."

He laughed and said, "Lucky for me!"

I told him his Uber was on its way. "What's an Uber?" he said. I gave him a quizzical look. "I'm from a really small town in Connecticut," he explained.

I told him the process, making sure he knew that the driver would know how to get there and that he wouldn't have to pay. When he arrived, he should just get out of the car and go inside the hotel to meet his uncle. I showed him the location of the car on my phone.

"Wow, it's close by already?"

I showed him the license plate number we were looking for. The car arrived and stopped on the other side of Arlington Street in front of the Taj. I waved and shouted, "Raoul! We'll come to you."

Getting in on the game, the kid also shouted, "Raoul!" Then he almost stepped out into traffic. I held him back and said, "Let's not die. That's not how this story ends."

We crossed the street to safety. As the kid was about to get into the back seat, I asked what his name was.

"Dylan."

"Well, Dylan, good luck and enjoy yourself in Boston."

I went to shake his hand but then he grabbed me. "I want to give you a hug. You saved me! Enjoy church."

"Don't get lost again," I called out as he closed the car door.

I felt immense joy being able to help this person, who needed so little from me but who needed it so very badly. I did my usual sprint to church and somehow made it just before the service started. My friends Ian and Stephen raised their eyebrows but I knew they would understand once they heard the story. Later I checked my phone, and saw that the Uber had made it to the destination. Only $8.28 and fifteen minutes of my time for an experience I will remember for a long time to come. And I knew he would always remember it as well.

As 2016 progressed, I realized that I needed to write something more substantial about my experience. I had no idea whether or not I would be able to do it but I knew that trying was the only way to find out. One day I was doing some research on vocal repertoire and

I learned that two famous sopranos I have admired and identified with, Arleen Auger and Lucia Popp, both died at the age of fifty-four, both from brain tumors, both in the same year (1993). After a day of feeling off-balance over the news, I felt new resolve to try to articulate how my brain tumor had changed me (and was continuing to change me each day). I wanted to learn from what happened to me, and to fully appreciate the ways in which my life was actually improved by the experience. I no longer wanted to wallow in the fear and uncertainty.

During that summer the book of Job popped up in the Daily Office Lectionary. Like so many other people, I have long found comfort and connection in this story. Job undergoes a multitude of losses—his property, his children—and it takes him an astonishingly long time to blame God: "Naked I came from my mother's womb, and naked shall I return there; the Lord gave, and the Lord has taken away; blessed be the name of God" (Job 1:21). But when he loses his health, he curses the day he was born. His friends try to comfort him and to assure him that God is still with him, but he doesn't believe them. He cries out and receives no answer, he says, and his friends can't put themselves in his place: "I cry to you, and you do not answer me; I stand, and you merely look at me" (Job 30:20). He cannot see any reason why God has forsaken him in this way, and why his fortunes have turned downward so precipitously. Essentially he is saying, "Why me?"

At last God answers Job, telling him that He has a few questions for him:

> Where were you when I laid the foundation of the earth?
> Tell me, if you have understanding.
> Who determined its measurements—surely you know?
>
> Job 38:4–5

God continues to list all of the natural phenomena He created in the world, and asks Job if he can control any of them: the rain, the mountains, the animals, the dawn, etc. Job is chastened, and replies,

> I know that you can do all things,
> and that no purpose of yours can be thwarted.
> Who is this that hides counsel without knowledge?
> Therefore I have uttered what I did not understand,
> things too wonderful for me, which I did not know.
>
> Job 42:2–3

In reading this book, I identify with Job's sense of unfairness in life and with his feelings of abandonment. And I have a similar emotional response to God's answer: it reminds me that the world is too great for me to understand, and my illnesses and other calamities are not for me to understand either. The world is a big, beautiful, complicated place, and its creation is far beyond my imagination. There is no way for me to comprehend why or how the gift of life was given to me, nor how long I will have the ability to enjoy that gift.

Somehow I never really railed against God in "Why me?" fashion, though perhaps I would have if I had been younger at diagnosis. By this point in life, I had seen enough suffering in the world to react more along the lines of "Why *not* me?" What was so special about me that I would be immune to this kind of illness? Ironically enough, I have also wondered "Why *not* me?" when I have despaired about my love life and my inability to find a lifelong partner. This is the area of my life about which I have railed angrily to God. I have been fortunate enough to cling closer to Him in the face of the brain tumor, not to feel as though He has turned His back on me. And yes, this is a lesson for me in the rest of my life.

As I gained the perspective of distance, I saw many bright moments that summer. I wept as I watched Hillary Rodham Clinton accept the Democratic nomination for President, the first woman to receive this honor. Months later I wept again as I stood in the voting booth to vote for her. It was beyond emotional to be able to cast a presidential ballot for a woman at long last. (Of course I have wept many times since that election for other reasons.)

I began to exhale as the months lengthened and I was still fine. One of my favorite verses became Ecclesiastes 9:7, which reads, "Go, eat your bread with enjoyment, and drink your wine with a merry heart; for God has long ago approved what you do." Life began to seem normal again, or at least a bit less fraught with emotion. The MRIs every four months began to feel *de rigueur,* like going to the dentist or taking my cat to the vet.

In September I joined an online brain tumor forum, hoping to have a place to take any fears that arose without burdening my friends and family. I quickly realized, however, that the posts on the forum were unfiltered, and I wouldn't have much ability to keep from receiving unwanted advice. One person messaged me with the dark advice that with every scan, the likelihood that the next one will go wrong increases over time, so I should use my money to go on holidays while I'm still healthy. Another woman with my same kind of tumor posted that she is thirty-four years old and would be overjoyed to see fifty, so I should be grateful that I have already reached that milestone birthday. I closed my account not long after reading those messages.

That fall our opera department produced *Hydrogen Jukebox,* Philip Glass's 1990 chamber opera on texts by the beat poet Allen Ginsberg. At the end of the piece, the cast sings Ginsberg's poem "Father Death Blues," which included these stanzas:

Genius Death	your art is done
Lover Death	your body's gone
Father Death	I'm coming home
Guru Death	your words are true
Teacher Death	I do thank you
For inspiring me	to sing this Blues

Two of my Opera Institute sopranos were in the piece, and our conductor advised me on the best place to sit because it was produced in the round. One of my sopranos was facing me directly, just feet away, when she looked me in the eye and sang the line, "Teacher Death I do thank you for inspiring me to sing this Blues." Tears rolled down my cheeks as I held my breath and tried to keep from sobbing audibly. When she sang, I just knew I was going to be okay. It was one of the most beautiful moments of my teaching life.

One of the best sermons I have ever heard was Father Sammy Wood's Easter Vigil sermon one year at The Church of the Advent. He noted that the darkness of Lent was over but many of us are still in darkness—marital problems, still waiting for the test results to come back, etc.—and need to remember that Christ is our light. Then he told a story about a fellow priest he knew named Mark. One morning in 2001 Mark's disabled adult son died suddenly while Mark was feeding him. His daughter lived in another state, and as Mark was driving to the airport to pick her up for the funeral, he saw the plane hit the Pentagon. After that he still came to church but didn't speak to anyone for months. Then one day he asked to address the congregation, and his final three words were, "The bottom holds."

I would need these words when I learned what 2017 would bring.

—6—
BASKETBALL

Bodies take real beatings. That they recover from most things is an underrated miracle.

—Barbara Brown Taylor

"Well, there's no sign of diverticulitis," the ER resident said.

"That's good, right?" I responded with a smile, hope fading rapidly as the resident slowly pulled a chair closer to my bed.

"We found a very large tumor attached to your adrenal gland," he said. "As soon as we can find a bed for you, we are going to admit you for further testing."

It was just a few days after Christmas 2016. I hadn't been feeling right for a few months. I first noticed weight gain during my trip to London in October (I was doing a mini-residency at the Royal College of Music). One evening I put on a London Fog raincoat I hadn't worn since the previous season, and the buttons wouldn't close properly. It was extremely tight just under my bra line, not down in the stomach area where I typically carry my extra weight. I didn't think anything dire other than this might be a new, depressing feature of the physical aging process.

During the few months following the London trip, I felt bloated, fat, and generally stressed out. The feeling of bloating came and went, so I attributed it to my varying intake of food and wine. I also noticed that my voice was taking longer than usual to warm up. Reflux can cause that to happen, so I thought it was just a normal result of my over-eating. (There is no limit to the self-blame we women can have, particularly around body image issues.) I also speculated that at the age of fifty-one, my vocal abilities might be starting to decline, and this thought added to my stress level (and my over-eating). In November, Donald J. Trump was elected President of the United States, and to me (and to at least half of the country), this felt like the end of the free world. Holiday tension ratcheted up in my family, not because we disagreed but because we were all so distraught. Given all of these obvious hammers on my emotional and physical health, I ignored my symptoms and never considered that this could be a tumor. I already had a brain tumor, and as I now knew, these don't metastasize to other parts of the body. And how could I possibly have developed another, unrelated problem?

By the end of December I found it impossible to lie on my stomach or sit down comfortably while wearing a belt. I remembered the perforated colon I had experienced just three years earlier and the pain I had ignored then. Once the Christmas rush ended, I decided it was finally time to get this checked. I called my primary care doctor's office, and they told me to go directly to the ER for imaging. As I waited in the ER, I listened to the drunk guy down the hall loudly singing over and over the old John Denver song, "Take Me Home, Country Road." Only he never progressed past the first few lines because he couldn't remember the words.

"Almost heaven, West Virginia, Blue Ridge Mountains, Shenandoah River . . ." he slurred over and over again.

"Life is old there, older than the trees!" I wanted to shout out.

When they rolled me in for the CT scan, I bantered with the tech about my brain tumor (techs like to know what else you already have) and my fear that I might have diverticulitis again. I'm an old pro at these scans now and I assumed I was just being overly cautious. I first sensed that something might be terribly wrong when he rolled me back out of the machine.

"Good luck to you," he said, unable to look me in the eye and all kidding manner gone. I knew he had seen something, but since technicians are prohibited by law from sharing scan results, he couldn't tell me anything.

It was almost midnight when I was taken by ambulance to another building on the Beth Israel campus. The young resident who checked me in there welcomed me to the OB-GYN oncology ward. I asked him why I was being admitted to OB-GYN when the tumor was on my adrenal gland.

"It's not on your adrenal gland," he said in a superior manner. "The truth is that it's so large—22 centimeters—that we can't tell exactly where it is attached. If it turns out to be cancerous, it would be defined as a cancer of whatever it grew from: the uterus, the ovaries, the appendix...."

"Ovarian cancer?" I interrupted.

"That is one of the possibilities on the list," he said casually. Then he saw my face and started backpedaling.

"We won't know anything until they run more tests. The surgeon will examine you in the morning. You should just try to get some rest."

Yeah, right.

How do you face the possibility of ovarian cancer just a few years after a brain tumor diagnosis? During that first night I was in a state of shock. I had just learned to live with the brain tumor and to see my life as better because of it. Now I had no idea what to expect. And of course, it never bodes well for the stability of your overall body chemistry when there is a second tumor, related or not. It was impossible for me to consider that I was spared a terminal diagnosis from the brain tumor only to go down with ovarian cancer.

In the morning I waited for the OB-GYN doctor in between frequent visits from nurses to take vital signs. Apologetically I ventured into the other half of the room to use the bathroom, where my roommate was a very kind older lady. She said she couldn't help overhearing that I was a teacher, and she asked me what I taught. Then she said something on which I hung for weeks: "Just remember, you don't have a diagnosis yet." I thanked her for her kindness and she replied, "If we can't be kind to one another in this world, what's the point?" Excellent question.

The OB-GYN doctor finally came to examine me. There's nothing quite like having a pelvic exam right there in your room, with people wandering past you in the hallway. The doctor said she didn't find anything out of the ordinary but they were concerned about the size of the tumor, especially because it had grown to this size in such a short time. They knew this because of the full-body scan I was given during my brain tumor treatment almost three years prior.

They decided not to operate immediately, saying they preferred to do a full work-up first. They would try to do the surgery laparoscopically but the tumor was likely too big for anything but open abdominal surgery. I should plan to be out of work for a minimum of six to eight weeks.

"My students will freak out!" was my first uncensored reaction.

"Can't someone else cover your classes?" the doctor said. I tried to explain the nature of what I do. Naively I somehow thought I could get this done and miss only a few weeks, like the last time. Again, I was trying to pretend everything was normal.

Since they had decided not to operate immediately, I was released from the hospital until the first working day after the holiday, when the testing could begin and I could be examined again. Happy New Year!

When I read my journal entries from the early days of the new tumor, I am struck by how positive I tried to be, even if I didn't feel it. I can hear my voice attempting to convince myself that everything would be fine:

Dec. 31, 2016

I am strong and I can get through this. It's unlikely that this new tumor will be anything but benign; these are fairly common and they're usually nothing. I know I will feel better when it's out and hopefully that will be the end of it. I will recover quickly. God is with me. And I have so many people praying with me. The size of it as they found it—22 cm.—is not lost on me. I know my dad is watching over me as well.

There's no need to go to Defcon 9 now. I have to assume it's benign and just focus on taking care of myself through surgery and recovery. I have the life skills to do this—I learned last time how to care for my mind and body in times like these.

The number twenty-two has special significance in my family. It was my father's basketball number, and he and my mother met on a church basketball team. Following my father's death in 2002, the number twenty-two started appearing in many seemingly random places. Most notably, I saw the number on an audience seat, under a bright spotlight, as I was rehearsing Barber's *Knoxville: Summer of 1915* one morning with the Abilene Philharmonic Orchestra. On the night of the performance, the house was extremely full, but no one was in that particular seat, and the light was still shining directly on it. So the size of the tumor seemed to me to be a message from my father that it was time for me to get this taken care of but that it would be fine. At least believing this helped me to remain calm.

New Year's Day 2017 happened to be a Sunday, and I attended the first mass without my beloved friends and seatmates Ian and Stephen. (They had left town that morning to move back home to Missouri, where Ian would successfully run for State Representative.) I sang the final descant with as much joy as I could find. At the end of the service Father Warren invited me to come to the rail for a blessing. He anointed my forehead with oil as he said in booming, deeply reassuring voice, "All sickness of mind and body take flight." Father Warren has one of those voices that removes all doubt and leads you to wonder if God himself is actually speaking directly to you.

On January 3, I received the excellent news that my blood did *not* show elevated levels of CA-125 (cancer antigen), the marker for ovarian cancer. My surgeon Dr. Liu described the tumor as "basketball-sized" but she believed it would prove to be "borderline" (in terms of malignancy) and the surgery should be the only treatment needed. The plan was to remove an impressive list of organs just to make sure nothing could grow back: all reproductive organs (uterus, Fallopian tubes, cervix), part of my omentum (abdominal fat pad), and possibly part of my intestines.

I was hopeful the last one would not be necessary, as it could mean I would need a colostomy bag. I had to give permission ahead of time for them to take that measure. I asked why I would ever consider saying no. Dr. Liu explained that some older women reach a point where they are just done with treatment and would rather not live than endure life with a colostomy bag. It was a sobering conversation despite her attempt to make it feel routine. At my age, the loss of my reproductive organs didn't faze me. It was worth it to me to ensure that I could never develop any of those cancers in the future.

Dr. Liu gave me permission to leave the next day on my annual trip to see friends in Texas since it would take a few weeks to arrange all of the tests I would need prior to surgery. I was in an odd limbo for a while but it was wonderful to spend time with friends instead of fretting alone. I visited my former church, where I spoke with many people about the surgery, including an older woman named Jo Patterson, who had always inspired me with her strength, intelligence, and grounded spirituality. She took my hand and said with her otherworldly calm, "God and I have talked about it, and it's going to be alright." She was so sure about it that my eyes filled with tears.

When I returned, the testing began: mammogram, another CT scan, and last but not least, a colonoscopy. They were looking for any other tumors before opening up my abdomen. All of these tests came back negative, which continued to put everyone at ease regarding my prognosis. I was reassured by the constant sense that this was a far more routine, less dangerous surgery than my brain surgery, because all of the health professionals around me behaved in a much less urgent way.

Outside of the hospital, I had many things to organize. At school we made arrangements for my leave of absence. Instead of the recommended four to six weeks, I arranged to be gone for just three and a half, and to have most (but not all) of the lessons covered by our fine vocal coaches (thanks again, Bill, Javier, and Michelle!). We also arranged for me to watch recordings of the auditions and score them at home, because I would miss all but one afternoon of the four full days. So many basketball jokes were made with close friends, rendered even more comical by the role of basketball in my family history. I sang one last Sunday with the Advent Choir, both mass and evensong, just days before the surgery. During the hymn "A Mighty Fortress is our God," I had to stop singing at the line, "The body they may kill; God's truth abideth still." It was an understandably emotional time.

On January 18, I presented myself for the surgery. All I could think about that day was being allowed to eat when it was over. Between the colonoscopy and the surgical prep, it had been about six days of liquid diet only, which just doesn't satisfy. My brother John came to Boston once again to accompany me to the hospital, where we sat in the surgery waiting room for over two hours due to a prolonged surgery just before mine. I sincerely thought I might expire from hunger, thus removing the need for the surgery.

My procedure lasted four and a half hours, even longer than my craniotomy. Things took longer than expected for a few reasons. They found a second, small tumor on my appendix, which John dubbed "Son of Frankenstein." The appendix then had to be removed. They also removed large amounts of scar tissue each of the organs had grown for protection from invading cells, which is a pretty amazing function of the human body. Dr. Liu told me the final size of the primary tumor was 40 cm. Since the anaesthesiologist had said it was 36 cm., and because this story was happening in New England, we made "Deflate-gate" jokes. Again I thought about the size at original diagnosis—22 cm.—and silently thanked my father. The basketball appeared to be filled with mucus, rather than tumor cells, so Dr. Liu said we would have to wait for the pathology report before we would know for sure what my condition was.

Alone in my room later that night I heard a voice from the next bed over. "Hi, I'm Lynn," she said from the other side of the curtain.

"No way. I'm Lynn too."

"Lynn with an E or no E?"

"No E. But my middle initial is E for Eleanor, so that confuses people," I said.

"No E for me either and my middle name is Ellen."

Over the days that I shared a room with Lynn, I learned that a sense of humor goes a long way in these situations, and that someone else always has a worse situation than you do. I never did determine exactly why she was in the hospital. She was bedridden and never came into my half of the room to use the bathroom. Doctors of all types came to see her about a seemingly endless list of conditions. But no one else came. She didn't have a single visitor in the three days we were roommates, nor did she receive any flowers or calls. There was never any discussion of how long she had been there, or when she might be discharged.

Despite all of that, she cheered me up over and over again. During the first day after the surgery, I became ill so the residents pulled my food again, this time not even allowing liquids, and said I might be able to go back to liquids the next day. I had a meltdown. I didn't see how starving would help me to recover, and I didn't care what vomiting might do to my open abdominal incision. All I wanted, I told one doctor, was an f-ing cracker (but I used the more coarse word). I was so hungry, tired, and scared that I was beyond all reason. Lynn encouraged me to speak to my nurses, she helped me to understand why they weren't letting me eat, and she generally sympathized with my situation. The next morning they finally decided to let me eat and the first crackers they brought tasted like heaven.

That Friday was the presidential inauguration, and Lynn's TV was tuned in loudly. I had been hoping not to see or hear any of it, so I was not pleased to hear Lynn repeatedly telling the nurses this was "a historic day." Then I heard her say something that made me laugh so hard my incision hurt.

"I'm just glad I'm already here in the hospital so that when he puts his hand on that Bible, you can revive me." We all laughed and then she and I commiserated about what a total disaster this was for our country.

When I received two flower arrangements and had various friends come to visit, I felt grateful but also sad for Lynn. My friend Jim brought me a Starbucks coffee and Lynn later told me that she "almost tackled him for it." She was a coffee fanatic and couldn't tolerate the awful hospital coffee. When I arranged for my friend Michelle to pick me up, I asked her to bring a coffee for Lynn. You would have thought I had given her a new car, she was so grateful. I also gave her one of my flower bouquets as I left.

I thought about her often in the following weeks and wondered how or if her medical journey had ended. I posted on Facebook about the woman who was so kind and funny and yet had no visitors or calls. Several of my friends said they were planning to send her cards. I hope for her sake that at least one of them did.

Back at home there was little to do but wait for the lab results and prepare to sit on the couch for three full weeks. I should have taken longer to recover, and I had to be cleared to go back to work before the full six weeks had passed, but I didn't want to miss so much of the semester. I also knew I would go insane at home for six weeks. As it was, I missed my student Wee Kiat Chia's performance in the

Metropolitan Opera New England Region finals, and I missed my friend Alice Coote's *Winterreise* at Zankel Hall in New York (having had tickets for that recital a full year in advance). Fortunately I had home visits from nurses to check my vitals as well as a steady stream of students, family, and friends. My almost-daughter Maddie picked up my prescriptions for me. I was especially grateful to my sister Jessica, who flew in for a weekend to help me with laundry, shopping, and cleaning. Sometimes you just need your sister. I watched and rated all of our voice auditions and answered far too many emails to call this a true sick leave. I did read a lot of books just for pleasure, one of my favorite pastimes. This liminal period was not nearly as frightening as the one following my brain surgery.

Dr. Liu called on January 30 to let me know that the tumor was in fact "borderline at most" and there was "no evidence of carcinoma." She recommended no further treatment beyond examinations and scans every three to six months for the next five years. I returned to work on February 10 for an afternoon of graduate auditions and then started back more or less full time on February 13.

One Sunday morning not long after my return to work, I was exhausted and sick and debating whether or not to make the effort to attend church. I was watching an old episode of *Judging Amy,* the one in which Amy's friend Greta finds religion after a cancer diagnosis and then dies suddenly. Amy asks her court officer/friend Bruce why he goes to church. At first he tells her there is no simple answer but then he says he figures he has three choices:

1. There is no God.
2. There is a callous God who doesn't care about bad things happening to people.
3. There is a benevolent God who is beyond my understanding.

Amy asks what makes him choose number three. He answers, "The look on my daughter's face when I put her to bed."

I went to church that day.

And I was glad.

This should be the end of the story: the happy ending, the one in which I sail away from this crisis and resume life as it was before with a giant smile on my face. That's not really how it happened. For a while I found this diagnosis, which was less serious and not truly life threatening, much harder to take than my brain tumor. I told my sister I was nostalgic for the time when all I had to worry about was the brain tumor. There was something so messy and unseemly about this tumor, being involved with my gastrointestinal and female organs, whereas brain tumors carry a certain clean romanticism (think Mysterious Movie Disease). I also felt that I had used all of my powers of deflection the first time around and could not fight this addition to the pile.

I spent too much time thinking about what this meant even though all of my doctors agreed that these tumors were completely unrelated to my brain tumor (that is not the direction in which these tumors spread). It didn't help to be told that the Tumor Board (yes, there is such a horribly named body) apparently did not agree on whether or not the basketball and the Son of Frankenstein were the same growth or two different ones, nor could they agree on which scenario was more threatening. One doctor thought I should have chemotherapy and another surgery immediately, and Dr. Liu explained that this would all have to be done at another hospital (if the team had concurred with the lone doctor). In either case, as my friend MJ says, I must have some really funky body chemistry. I did my best to soldier on and to hide my fears from my loved ones.

Then at the beginning of March, just a few weeks after I returned to teaching, we received the shocking news that my esteemed voice colleague Jerrold Pope had died suddenly. I first met Jerry in fall 1995 at Florida State University, where I was a new doctoral student and he was a new assistant professor. He was one of the first people to encourage me as a teaching colleague, and he invited me to perform alongside him on a faculty recital there. When he left FSU, he let me know, and he was the main reason I came to Boston University. No one on the planet will ever know as much vocal repertoire as Jerry did, and he was endlessly generous with his encyclopedic knowledge. No one had a drier sense of humor at auditions either. We shared so many stories about my own teacher at FSU, who is a prodigiously talented character in her own right. To say this news hit me (and all of us) hard would be a major understatement. At this writing, we are still dealing with the effect of losing our brilliant, hilarious, superior colleague.

As I tried to incorporate this loss into everything else happening that winter, I caught some other curveballs. My insurance company opted not to cover this adventure as fully as they had covered the brain tumor treatment. Whereas that situation cost me roughly $300, this one cost me the full out-of-pocket deductible, $2500. I had two MRIs scheduled in April—head and abdominal—and I tried not to worry about the results or the cost. And then in May my beloved cat Jeoffrey, whom I'd had for all of his thirteen years, died very quickly from cancer.

There were some things that helped me to hold it together and to keep from spending all my time wallowing in "Why me?" territory. My performance of the Soprano I solos in the Mozart *C-Minor Mass* at Tufts (with one of my favorite conductors, Jamie Kirsch) went terrifically well. The Easter Vigil sermon given by Father Sammy reminded me that "the bottom holds." The April MRIs were both fine. I didn't make it through my tribute at Jerry's memorial without crying but my colleague Jim Demler read the rest of my written words for me. My students buoyed me every day with their kindness, their talent, and their youthful optimism.

I put aside this writing, though, because I was no longer in the emotional place I had planned to explore on paper. I couldn't honestly say my life was better because of this additional tumor. I felt like a fraud, because this benign abdominal tumor made me question everything I thought I had internalized about life. But this is how life works: the moment you think you have things figured out, you are probably due for a major kick in the pants. I prepared for a summer of licking my wounds and trying to put all of these health worries in the rear view mirror.

There's nothing quite as medicinal as time with like-minded friends and musical colleagues to put you back on the path. MaryJean Allen and Shannon McGinnis are two fine human beings and musicians with whom I worked at the Up North Vocal Institute for a number of years. MJ is a voice and Alexander Technique teacher with serious skills as well as the big sister I never had. Shannon is a superior coach/pianist, and when we team-taught, we joked that we were bad cop *and* bad cop because we both had such high standards for our singers. The three of us had been talking about creating some kind of workshop together for years and now it was about to become a reality.

I flew to Chicago in early June for our "Emerge!" weekend, sponsored by the Collaborative Arts Institute of Chicago. We chose the name to reflect our mission, which was to help young professional singers emerge from the crowded field by identifying their most unique talents. The structure of the weekend with our first group of six singers flowed exactly as we had envisioned it. Our three-way master class on the final afternoon was easy and collaborative. This sounds simple enough, but ask any musician you know how difficult it might be to teach a public class with more than one leader. Realizing this dream was deeply restorative to me (and I think to MJ and Shannon as well). Helping young people grow and succeed is what makes teaching such a satisfying career.

Teaching has always been the most effective way for me to get out of my own worrisome head and to contribute something to the greater good. I know that when I'm teaching, I'm focused on the student in front of me, not on my own problems or insecurities. While I enjoy performing, I don't have the same feeling about it in terms of helping anyone. I'm glad at least some of my students feel they have gotten something from me because I so often feel like I should be paying them for the privilege. I learn just as much, if not more, from them as they learn from me. Each and every one of the students I have worked with has changed me in some important way. I went back to Michigan that June for another summer on the faculty at the Up North Vocal Institute. Shannon and her husband rented a boat for the Fourth of July holiday, and they graciously invited me, MJ, and our friend Matthew Gemmill out on it for the afternoon. It was a perfect day in all respects: the weather, the scenery, the company, and the celebratory atmosphere. The boat came with equipment for tubing, and we all watched from the boat while Michael flew behind us on the tube. Shannon didn't want to go out on the tube alone and asked if anyone else would join her.

"I'll go," I said, standing up. Everyone stared at me.

"You will?" Michael said after a long moment.

"Yes, let's do this," I said, already losing a little of my nerve but determined to see it through. I am an introverted, highly cerebral person, not the kind of person to leap to a physical challenge. All of the illnesses I had experienced threatened to make me even less confident about my body. But that day I decided I should grab life by the tube and get out there.

Gracelessly I climbed down the back of the boat with my life jacket on and tried to lie down on my stomach next to Shannon on the tube. The minute the boat took off we slid right off the tube, our legs and lower bodies dangling in the wind behind us while we clung to the tube handles, screaming and laughing at the same time. MJ took a picture of us, and the only thing I don't love about that photo is that there's no audio.

That day felt like an emotional turning point for me, a day on which I decided to put aside fear (especially physical fear) and to embrace a day spent with four beloved friends. The day was enough in and of itself, and it didn't matter what else might happen later. I started to wonder if I could be enough for myself, not just that day but every day.

One of my favorite podcasts is The Hilarious World of Depression, hosted by John Moe. In one episode marked "placebo," listeners provided names of songs that helped them get through times of sadness. One listener brought the Peter Gabriel song, "Solisbury Hill." As soon as he said the name of the song, I know which line he would choose to highlight: "Grab your things, I've come to take you home." This line makes me feel both sad and happy. I love the idea that someone can take you out of the temporary place you've been in, not knowing it was not your permanent home, and bring you to the place you were supposed to be. I began to feel that I could choose a different place to live emotionally. The latest tumor was a derailment of limited duration, and I could find my way back to the better place, the better home I had made for myself after the brain tumor diagnosis. I remembered something Father Sammy said not long after his mother passed away. I had asked him if today was a good day, and he replied, "They're all good days."

By Thanksgiving I had successfully delivered all of my fall performances (the premiere and my recitals at Bucknell and Boston Universities) and I was ready to push worry aside again. "And can any one of you by worrying add a single hour to your span of life?" (Luke 12:25). On Thanksgiving Day, I copied down another verse followed by a list:

> And there will be no more night; they need no light of lamp or sun, for the Lord God will be their light, and they will reign forever and ever.
>
> Revelation 22:5

I have so many things to be thankful for:
- my health
- my family (& kitties)
- my friends everywhere
- my church
- my profession & students
- my apartment
- my financial security
- books and music

As the anniversary of my abdominal tumor (and the fourth anniversary of my brain tumor) approached, I fought off dark memories and fears, some days more successfully than others. Spending time at The Advent with my church family was an enormous source of strength and continuity. I kept trying to stay focused on helping others, especially my students, and to ward off anxiety and feelings of being overwhelmed. My daily task was to maintain a balance between work and taking care of myself, both emotionally and physically; my students call this "adulting." I learned that this was all easier if I could see myself as part of a community and to understand that I'm certainly not alone in my feelings. I continued to seek out books and podcasts authored by people facing major health issues.

Kate Bowler is an assistant professor at the Duke Divinity School, a wife and the mother, who was diagnosed with stage IV colon cancer. Her blog and podcast eventually took the form of a book called *Everything Happens for a Reason (And Other Lies I've Loved)*. Prior to her diagnosis, her research focused on the prosperity gospel. Loosely defined, this is the belief that God wants us to be materially successful, and anything negative, including illness, is evidence of weak faith. During my own year teaching at a small Baptist college, I encountered people who believe this.

Dr. Bowler's writings and podcasts are filled with humanity, compassion, thoughtfulness, and courage. I was moved by what she had to say about Christians:

> What if *rich* didn't have to mean *wealthy*, and *whole* did not have to mean *healed*? What if being people "of the gospel" meant that we are simply people with good news? God is here. We are loved. It is enough.

I identified with so many of her experiences and drew much strength from her joyful, personable communication style. She describes her cancer as the "second-least-sexy cancer" (behind rectal cancer). She writes of feeling frustrated when old people complain about their ailments because chances are high that she will not have a long life in which to decline physically. Like me, she felt compelled to keep working full days in order to hide her reality, not seeing at first that "surrender is not weakness." She writes with laser accuracy about some of the ways people behave toward her actually being worse than the cancer: minimizing her fears, telling her this must be teaching her something, or encouraging her to save herself by having a positive attitude. Dr. Bowler is more articulate about all of these feelings than I can be here. As she writes:

> Perhaps the weirdest thing about having something
> awful happen
> Is the fact that no one wants to hear about it.....
> Simmer down
> and
> Let them talk for a bit. Be willing to stare down the
> ugliness and Sadness. Life is absurdly hard, and pretending it
> isn't is exhausting.

I rounded out the Year of the Basketball with much introspection and a focus on closing this chapter in order to be able to see what might be next. "This is my comfort in my distress, that your promise gives me life," I copied from the book of Psalms (119:50). With help from a dear friend, I made a list in my journal:

I love myself.

I choose myself.

> I don't need to apologize for being human.
>
> I don't need anyone's approval to be here.
>
> I am loved by many, especially my family.

The holidays were filled with friends and family gatherings, but this year I added a few rituals for myself. On Christmas Eve I was the only one who wanted to go to church so I found a Service of Carols starting at 5:00 at the local Episcopal Church. At first I felt a little sad and conspicuous sitting alone on Christmas Eve. But people sat down near me and we sang all of the beloved carols. My heart lightened as I felt the familiar comfort of the Mass liturgy. I was renewed for the family dinner that followed.

The other new ritual was a New Year's Eve "Closing the Books for 2017." I made a long list of everything that happened during this tumultuous year, events both joyful and challenging, and said goodbye to each one as I remembered it once more. I was surprised by how many wonderful things there were to include. It is easy to let our concept of time be overtaken by large, stressful events, and to forget all of the many smaller gifts that make up the daily movie of our lives. I realized that my strength had been tested again but also that I had prevailed again. I felt ready to resume writing about the silver linings.

And now let us believe in a long year that is given to us, new, untouched, full of things that have never been, full of work that has never been done, full of tasks, claims, and demands.

Rainer Maria Rilke

Be strong and courageous; do not be frightened or dismayed, for the Lord your God is with you wherever you go.

Joshua 1:19

—7—
LESSONS

I slept in a bed
in a room with paintings
on the walls, and
planned another day
just like this day.
But one day, I know
it will be otherwise.

—JANE KENYON

We all know intellectually that one day we will stop breathing but we tend to live in denial of that reality because to dwell on it would paralyze us. We can't spend our lives in fear and sadness, waiting for our deaths. But how do we balance acceptance of our eventual demise with a healthy perspective, one in which we take nothing for granted, in which we waste no time in self-destructive behaviors?

The world is full of books, movies, music, and art telling us how to find the meaning of life. Don't worry, be happy. You only live once. Seize the day. Live like you're dying. Live like you mean it. Live life to the fullest. Be all that you can be. Always look on the bright side of life. Everything happens for a reason. Or as my dad used to say, there are no moving vans behind hearses.

I don't have anything new to add to this pile of aphorisms, nor would I presume to have any insider advice on how anyone else should live out their precious days here on earth. All I can do is share how this absolutely horrible experience has made my life happier. And then try to remember these lessons each and every day that I'm still here.

My faith has been a lamp on this path, and I have come to understand that faith is a living, evolving thing. The Anglican catechism says that the purpose of life is to glorify God and enjoy one's life. Often it feels like these things should be easier to accomplish than they are. How do we glorify God when terrible things befall us and our loved ones? How do we enjoy our lives when we are sick, lonely, and afraid? There are no simple answers and yet it is in the simplest things that we find answers. The major difficulties of life strip away the noise of our lives and reveal the bare bones construction of our public identities. We are relegated to smaller gestures, and we are forced to learn how to take pleasure in the smallest things. When the clouds dissipate, and they almost always do, we experience fuller joy than ever before.

As a lifelong musician, I have often felt that music and faith are one and the same. Music is a calling, not a job, and most musicians consider it a primary portion of our sense of self. It is not separate. We could never imagine turning our backs on it entirely, even when we are frustrated. We have spiritual experiences listening to and making music. It's one of the reasons we are particularly moved when we create or hear music in one of the world's great cathedrals. Music expresses faith and faith allows the music to happen.

I tell my students that singing a high note is an act of faith. Through technical practice and intentional use of the body, we create the optimal conditions in which the high note can blossom. And then we have faith that it will. Daily life is also an act of faith. We step out into the world and hope that most things will go according to plan, or at least that we will return home safely again in the evening.

In thinking about my life in a new light, I have considered what the purpose of music, particularly singing, can possibly be in a life so inherently precarious. What is my voice for? What is art for? Why do I have a singing voice and what should I do with it? Why should I teach anyone else to sing? I have certainly become less worried about performing; I only sing when I have something to say now, and I care quite a bit less about "perfection" and my image in the eyes of others. I know that the music I sing helps to frame my life and can help my listeners to frame their own experiences. I am a conduit for the poetry of other artists and nothing more. My students are the most important musical investment in my life now. I hope that their time with me has enriched their lives in return.

I have also spent a great deal of time thinking about luck and how having it or not changes our lives. In the music profession we learn early that luck plays a critical role in success. One must be ready to capitalize on a stroke of good luck but there is no denying that it may never come to us, and that it may strike the person next to us instead. In life it is much harder to accept these lottery-level odds.

We think we are sailing our own boats until something like this happens. And sometimes we can't see whether our luck is good or bad, at least not immediately. When I was initially diagnosed, I didn't see how fortunate I was to have been diagnosed so early, to be in Boston when it happened, to have the right chromosome, and ultimately to have one of the milder forms of brain tumors. All I heard was the shocking sound of the words "brain tumor."

At this writing it has been over six years since my diagnosis. Will I see another five years, or even another ten? No one knows. My tumor could remain dormant for decades or it could upgrade itself to an untreatable cancer at any time. Or I could die from something else today. Just ask the families of the nearly three thousand people who went to work on September 11 and never came home whether their loved ones expected what was coming.

In 2016 Joe Biden's advisors warned him that losing the primary as a sitting Vice President would be a big loss, and he should consider his legacy if he chose to run and was unsuccessful. But Biden had learned a valuable lesson following the death of his son Beau: "I understood the difference between an electoral loss and real loss. I wasn't afraid of losing a political race."

The brain tumor has taught me a similar lesson about fear. There are things I don't fear anymore, like giving a less than perfect performance or inadvertently saying something less than considered. I used to be physically unadventurous, afraid that people would laugh at me if I wasn't perfect. Recently I attended a Zumba class outside on the Charles River Esplanade by myself. I almost bailed because of potential embarrassment. But as I danced awkwardly in the sun with two hundred other awkward souls, all having the time of their lives, I realized that no one cared how stupid I looked. Everyone was just trying to sail their own boat, and no one was watching me. I would have missed out on one of the most enjoyable, freeing evenings of my life. And I made another addition to the list of Things I Would Never Have Done Before the Brain Tumor.

Control has been another major lesson from this experience, namely, the shedding of the illusion that I actually have any. I used to make myself sick with worry as I tried to control my environment. I was always looking five steps down the road for potential roadblocks. It's one of the traits that has served me well as a teacher and an administrator, professions in which an ability to see the big picture can be quite useful. But in taking the long view exclusively, I was depriving myself of all of the smaller moments of joy, and of all the listening I needed to do to the person right in front of me. You can't be a good listener when your brain is thinking about next week, next month, and next year.

I cannot deny that I occasionally have dark nights of the soul during which I foresee the end coming sooner rather than later, and ponder the shape the end might take. But these nights have also helped me to grow and adapt, because they have taught me how strong my faith is and how tightly connected I am to other people in the world. There are family members, friends, colleagues, and students who care about me, and there are other people I don't know who are going through something similar. This book is for all of those people.

ACKNOWLEDGEMENTS

This book has been in process for almost seven years now. I started making notes for it upon diagnosis and began writing in earnest a few months later. The second diagnosis derailed things for a while, so I am deeply grateful to all who helped me push the book across the finish line.

I must begin with the folks at GIA, most especially with Alec Harris for his continuing support of my work. Thank you, Alec, for believing in this particular book even though it falls a few stone's throws away from my other writing. I want to thank my longtime friend and mentor James Jordan for encouraging my career from the beginning, and also for the *kintsugi* analogy. Thanks as well to my editor Kirin Nielsen for her work on this project. I am greatly appreciative of my big sister MaryJean Allen, both for her eagle eye on my manuscript and her generous comments for the back cover. Thank you also, Craig Terry, for your thoughtful words of endorsement. I must thank another longtime friend and mentor, Lois Svard, for writing the beautiful foreword, and for her advice and support throughout all of these years.

I would not be here to write this if it weren't for my astonishing medical team at Beth Israel: Dr. Ron L. Alterman, who performed my brain surgery; Dr. Fong W. Liu, who performed my abdominal surgery; Dr. Christopher Stephen, who provided calm guidance during my initial hospital stay; "Mike from Radiology" and all of the nurses and techs who walked me through everything; Kate Nolan, my nurse practitioner; and Leah Bass, my therapist. And most of all, for Dr. Erik J. Uhlmann, my neuro-oncologist, whose gentle kindness and clear explanations continue to shine light on my path.

I am fortunate to have a close network of friends all over the country who sustain me. For my dear friends in New York: Kevin Murray, Matthew Horner, Chris O'Neill, Dan Tepfer, Mark Heimbigner, and Bill Ames; for my Ohio friends Kevin Jones, Joe Bellissimo, and all the folks at First Congregational Church in Columbus; for my dear church family at The Advent, Ian Mackey, Stephen Eisele, Father Sammy Wood, Mark Dwyer, Jeremy Bruns, Elise and Matt Groves, John Ross Campbell, Phillip Shearin, Ignacio Gama, Ross Wood, Michael Oliveri, Eric Aho, Father Douglas Anderson, Jeff and Roxy Hanson, and the lovely members of the Advent Women's Group; for my Bucknell friends, especially Devon Bakum, William Payn, and Brian Nedvin, and for my friends from the UNVI days, especially Shannon McGinnis, David Thesenga, Matthew Chellis, and Matthew Gemmill. Wishing you all lots of wine and popcorn.

For friends in other places far and near: Nicholas Sears, James Whitbourn, Hugh Russell, Michelle Alexander, Sarah Thaxton Miller, Sonya Baker, Todd Wilson, Jeffrey Picon, Troy Peters, Matt Glandorf, Alan Morrison, David Mallette, Larry Stotsbery, and Doug Fisher; and my Texas friends, Kay and Paul Camp, Nicholas Williams, Donna Emmanuel, Michael and Cindy Cooper, Heidi and Joe Klein, Jeffrey Snider, Beth Jackson, Rhonda Thomas, Fred and Jo Patterson, Jeannette Ceballos, Richard and Katherine Sparks, Warren Henry, and Richard Croft.

Boston University has been wonderfully supportive toward me during these years. I appreciate my friends and colleagues there who made things easier: William Lumpkin, Allison Voth, Gregory Melchor-Barz, Ruthie Jean, Shiela Kibbe, McCaela Donovan, Harvey Young, Benjamin Juarez, Patricia Mitro, Stephanie Mao, Aaron Sheehan, Victor Coelho, Michelle LaCourse, Terry Everson, Oshin Gregorian, Matthew Larson, Barbara Raney, Jill Pearson, Mary Ducharme, Karin Hendricks, Tawnya Smith, Andrew Goodrich, Kinh Vu, Diana Dansereau, Clera Ryu, Ben Court, James Sparks, and Bramwell Tovey. And for the members of the voice department who share my boat with such good humor every day, Penelope Bitzas, Sharon Daniels, James Demler, Phyllis Hoffman, Douglas Sumi, and our newest colleague David Guzman.

To my dear students: I can't thank you enough for your kindness, your patience, and your laughter when I needed it most. For allowing me to include your experience, I am especially grateful to Mary Conley. Special thanks also to Madeline Radway, Caroline Camp Corrales, Kelley Hollis, Helen Hassinger, Ruby White, Arielle Rae Basile, Jenni Klauder, Maayan Harel, Kathryn Tolley, Joshua Dixon, Chris MacRae, Cara Grimaldi, Erika Anderson, Kristin Howard, Katie Tiemeyer, Caroline Bourg, Tara Dougherty, Noah Fischer, Lily Balshan, Bryan Pollock (and Meng Kang), Wee Kiat Chia (and Joshua Stone), Julianne Wolfe, Erik Danielson, Kyuyoung Lee, Kat Middeldorp, Lu Tan, Adriana Nieves, Emily Jaworski, Heather Hawk, Jennifer Ciobanu, Drew Nelson, Logan Walsh, Kristen Bigham, Jennifer Harvey, Jennifer Romig, Erika Rajkovic, Alecia Batson, Anna Ward, Lydia McClain, Cody Bowers (and Tony Pastor), Dennis Shuman, Olivia Ericsson, and Rose Lewis.

Most of all, this book is for my beloved family. Because of the love and care of my brother John Eustis, my sister Jessica Eustis Oakhem, my mother Carole Eustis, my sister-in-law Beth McDermott Eustis, my brother-in-law Strider Oakhem, my nephews Thomas Gunning, Noah Eustis, and Jake Oakhem, and my nieces Lola Eustis and Grace Oakhem, I know I am never alone in the world. How lucky I am to have all of you in my life, and to know the peace that comes with unconditional love.

RECOMMENDED FURTHER READING

Memoirs specific to brain tumors

Biden, Joe. *Promise Me, Dad: A Year of Hope, Hardship, and Purpose.* (New York: Flatiron Books/Macmillan, 2017)

Blain, Adam. *Pear Shaped: The Funniest Book So Far This Year About Brain Cancer.* (Self-published on CreateSpace Independent Publishing Platform, 2015)

Gunther, John J. *Death Be Not Proud.* (New York: Harper Perennial Modern Classics, 1949/2007)

Purmott, Nora McInerny. *It's Okay to Laugh: (Crying is Cool Too).* (New York: Dey Street Books/HarperCollins, 2017)

Ziegler, Deborah. *Wild and Precious Life.* (New York: Atria/Emily Bestler Books/Simon & Schuster, 2016)

Books by Neurosurgeons

Black, Peter. *Living with a Brain Tumor: Dr. Peter Black's Guide to Taking Control of Your Treatment.* (Griffin, 2006)

Black, Keith. *Brain Surgeon: A Doctor's Inspiring Encounters with Mortality and Miracles* (Grand Central Life and Style, 2016).

Marsh, Henry. *Admissions: Life as a Brain Surgeon.* (Thomas Dunne Books, 2017)

Marsh, Henry. *Do No Harm: Stories of Life, Death, and Brain Surgery.* (New York: Picador/Macmillan, 2016)

Taylor, Lynne P. *Navigating Life with a Brain Tumor.* (Oxford, UK: Oxford University Press, 2012)

Memoirs about terminal illness

Bowler, Kate. *Everything Happens For a Reason: And Other Lies I've Loved.* (New York: PenguinRandom House, 2018)

Kalanithi, Paul. *When Breath Becomes Air.* (New York: Random House, 2016)

Riggs, Nina. *The Bright Hour: A Memoir of Living and Dying.* (New York: Simon & Schuster, 2018)

Other

Gawande, Atul. *Being Mortal: Medicine and What Matters in the End.* (New York: Picador/Macmillan 2015)

Gawande, Atul. *Better: A Surgeon's Notes on Performance.* (New York: Picador/Macmillan, 2008)

Kenyon, Jane. *Collected Poems.* (Minneapolis, MN: Graywolf Press, 2007)

Taylor, Jill Bolte. *My Stroke of Insight: A Brain Scientist' Personal Journey.* (London, UK: Penguin Books, 2009)

Transue, Emily. *On Call: A Doctor's Days and Nights in Residency.* (New York: Griffin/Macmillan 2005)

ABOUT THE AUTHOR

Lynn Eustis is a brain tumor survivor and faculty member at Boston University, where she teaches voice. She is the author of *The Singer's Ego* and *The Teacher's Ego*. A native of Long Island, New York, she lives in Boston with her two cats.